Advice for Today
Tomorrow
& Forever

Timeless Wisdom for You and Your Family

ILYNMW Publishing
Atlanta Georgia

Dedication

This book is dedicated to my Bride and the love of my life - Debbie. I also want to dedicate this book to my children - Hannah, David, Sarah and Jonathan. I am so proud of you guys and I love you no matter what!

Books by Paul Beersdorf

Flowers on Tuesday

52 Things I Wish My Father Had Taught Me about Marriage and Family

The 100 Most Important Words

Encouraging Your Wife

Encouraging Your Husband

Contents

Acknowledgements

I love my Bride of how much she encourages me to write and share my thoughts and ideas. She is the love of my life and my best friend. Nothing I do would be worthwhile without her by my side. I would also like to thank my many friends and family who have reviewed this book and offered their thoughts, wisdom and advice.

No book is ever written by a single author. There is always a group of people who help to make the final product more complete and useful.

Introduction

Advice comes from many quarters in our life; friends, family, co-workers, strangers, books, the internet, and many other places.   All of these sources seem to offer advice on just about every aspect of life.   However, what is good advice and what is bad advice?

Unsolicited advice is probably the worst type of advice! Even if it is good, it will probably be ignored, or at worst be counterproductive.

Truly bad advice can come from the foolish or ignorant person who is not trying to intentionally do you harm, but just does not know any better. Bad advice can come from good people who make poor choices and are blinded by their own situation.   Or worse yet is the person who gives you bad advice with the clear intention of watching you fail.

Now that 2/3 of my life is over (based on current actuarial tables), I reflect on my life and the advice and wisdom that have been poured into me.   I have been blessed to have so many wise and intelligent people in my life who have wanted me to succeed and do well.

Some of the advice in this book is very practical, some is profound and some is just funny.   As you read, please make sure to note the quotes in each section. There is much profound and timeless wisdom from some of the most brilliant minds.   In addition, the bible verses that accompany most of the chapters offer insight and wisdom from God's point of view.

This book is my attempt to capture as much of this advice in one place for my children and my children's children. Some of this advice is original, but most has been passed down from generation to generation. If I can remember who the advice came from, then I will give them credit, but much of this advice is stuff I have written down or heard over the years and I don't always know who to credit.   I certainly do not claim credit for myself and apologize in advance for not knowing the source.

Finally, I think it is important to point out the difference between wisdom and knowledge

Knowledge is about facts and figures.   How many ounces in a pound? Who won the Superbowl last year? What is the speed of light in a vacuum?

Wisdom however is about knowing:

- When to say YES or NO
- When to speak and when to listen
- When to encourage and when to admonish
- When to start and when to stop
- When to invest and when to save
- When to push and when to pull
- When to give and when to take

Wisdom is all about decision making.

Lots of people have knowledge, very few people have wisdom. Determine now to seek wisdom and discernment.

My hope is that this book will be a blessing to you and your family.

Legal Disclaimer

I received some advice that it would be a good idea to include a legal disclaimer. So, out of an abundance of caution, I have included the following legal disclaimer.

I am not a lawyer, certified financial planner, accountant or any other kind of financial advisor. You should seek professional advice before you make any legal decisions or financial investment decisions. Everyone's situation is unique and should be treated as such.

The information provided in this book and accompanying material is for informational purposes only. It should not be considered legal or financial advice. You should consult with an attorney or other professional to determine what may be best for your individual needs.

I do not make any guarantee or other promise as to any results that may be obtained from using this content. No one should make any investment decision without first consulting his or her own financial advisor and conducting his or her own research and due diligence. To the maximum extent permitted by law, I disclaim any and all liability in the event any information, commentary, analysis, opinions, advice and/or recommendations prove to be inaccurate, incomplete or unreliable, or result in any investment or other losses.

Content made available through this book is not intended to and does not constitute legal advice or investment advice and no attorney-client relationship is formed. Your use of the information in this book is at your own risk.

Ok, now that we have that out of the way, we can proceed!

Advice for Today Tomorrow & Forever

Timeless Wisdom for You and Your Family

Top 10 Pieces of Advice

I know many people will not venture to read this entire book. Therefore, I wanted to offer 10 pieces of advice that would encapsulate my entire body of learning, research and knowledge.

Trying to get these down to 10 is pretty tough. I wanted to make sure that I cover the key areas of a person's life where most of us need advice and or struggle.   These top 10 include - spiritual, financial, physical, mental, and relational advice.

The advice below is broad enough in scope to cover a multitude of situations, but specific enough to be clearly understood.   The first two items are foundational to your entire life and being.   If you strive to achieve the first two items on this list, then it will make your decision making about the other items much easier.

1.   **Love God with all your heart, mind, body and soul**

2.   **Love your neighbor as yourself**

3.   **Invest your time wisely**

4.   **Never borrow money**

5.   **Spend less than you make**

6.   **Save, save, save & Give Generously**

7.   **Never stop learning**

8.   **Be prepared**

9.   **Attitude is everything**

10. **Take care of your body**

As I did research for this book, I found a number of articles about advice from 100 year old people. I can juxtapose the top ten on the previous page with a recap of what appears to me to be the top 10 pieces of advice from these 100 year old folks (in no particular order).

1. Watch what you eat & exercise

2. Spend more time with family and friends

3. Don't let things bother you (stop worrying).

4. Have a positive attitude

5. Have an active sense of humor and laugh a lot

6. Open and honest communication

7. Keep your mind active

8. Be content

9. Be wise with your money

10. Learn to forgive

Not a bad list at all! To me the overall theme from the elderly is CHILL OUT! They have learned that life is not nearly as serious as we make it. We waste a lot of time on worthless activities. People are important! Time and energy should be spent investing into and building those relationships.

Finally, I would like to close out this section by looking at the top 10 pieces of advice from the wisest man in the world.

God gave Solomon wisdom unlike anyone before him or after him. The wisdom that God gave to Solomon amazed those around him and even had leaders from around the world come to sit with him and hear his wisdom.

In the book of Proverbs, we have 31 chapters of wisdom that Solomon recorded. While I am no Bible scholar, I have been reading the book of Proverbs for decades now and it is amazing how fresh and relevant the advice is today as it was thousands of years ago.

Below is my attempt to list what I believe are the top 10 pieces of advice that Solomon had to offer (in no particular order).

1. **Seek wisdom and understanding**

2. **Watch what you say**

3. **Watch what you eat and drink**

4. **Beware of the company you keep**

5. **Be faithful to your spouse, avoid sexual immorality**

6. **Avoid laziness, be diligent**

7. **Listen to your parents**

8. **Be careful with money and wealth**

9. **Humility is more powerful than pride**

10. **Seek wise counsel for decisions**

The key words that come up again and again in the book of Proverbs speak to the priorities that Solomon wanted to convey:

Wisdom
Work
Understanding
Trust
Patience
Love
Humility
Honor
Honesty
Discipline
Diligence

Money

I am starting this book with my advice on Money. This is a subject that is relevant anywhere, anytime with anybody. Money is something that we have to deal with from a young age until the day we die. We will never get away from it and if we are not careful, it will control us instead of us controlling it.

Please remember that I am just a father offering up advice and I am not a lawyer, financial planner or accountant. This is just advice that has worked for me and my situations in life.

Caveat - When I use calculations, I will be keeping things very simple. This is not meant to be a complete study in finance. It is about practical advice.

I have broken down this chapter into the following sections:

- Saving
- Borrowing Money/Debt
- Retirement
- Spending
- Investing
- Giving
- Other

Saving

Save money by cooking meals at home

It is almost always less expensive to cook meals at home than it is to eat out. This is especially true for families with children. Invest your money in a Slow Cooker (Crockpot®) and you save both time and money on meals. Invest in a good cookbook and recipes.

Save money by taking your lunch to work

I have many friends at work who eat in the company cafeteria and do not even give a second thought to how much money they are spending on meals. The average lunch is about $6.00 in our cafeteria. That works out to $30 each week or about $1,500 per year for lunch. You can take your own lunch each day for about $1.50-$2.00 (a lot less if you only fix PB&J, an apple or banana and some chips/pretzels). The trick is to buy a big bag of pretzels or chips and then repack them into a smaller bag.

The difference is $4.00 per day or $20.00 per week. This works out to $1,000 per year. Assuming you are going to work about 40 years, that would be $40,000. Start small by taking lunch one day a week to start.

Save money by making your own coffee or tea

It cost next to nothing to make your own cup of coffee. If you spend just $2.00 per day on coffee, that is $14.00 per week or $728 per year for coffee. Spend $4.00 per day on coffee and now you are up to $1,456 per year on coffee. That works out to $58,240 over 40 years for coffee.

Teach your children to save at a young age

Don't just give you children things (that is too easy to do). Teach them at a young age to work and do chores and save their money. . It offers them the chance to learn patience as they save to buy that special item they want. Finally, they learn that it is their responsibility to earn money for things they want, and that the money tree of mom and dad is not everlasting.

Have several types of emergency funds:

Basic repairs and replacements, unexpected medical bills, emergency's, short term unemployment are just a few of the surprises life throws at us. You should have at minimum $1,000-$1,500 cash on hand to cover these type of expenses.

In addition, over time you will want to have saving to cover larger unexpected expense, such as long term loss of a job or extended medical care. A good rule of thumb is 6 to 12 months of expenses in emergency savings. You can easily calculate the amount needed by reviewing those basic expenses you will need to cover - rent/mortgage, utilities, transportation, and food.

You will not get there overnight, but saving some each month towards this amount will get you there. At the very minimum, try to have 3 months of expenses in savings.

Save money for college

This probably sounds too simple, but start saving early with a 529 plan (this is a special saving account for college that allows you to save money tax free). Start saving when you children are first born and by the time they are 18, you should have plenty of money saved. Many plans allow you to set up automatic savings each month so you never miss the money coming out of your account. In addition, you can ask family and friends to also contribute money to the 529 plan as well.

Save money by going to a community or local College for the first 2 years

You can save a ton of money by attending a local college for the first two years. Your saving will come from living at home and not paying for dorm/apartment and all the living expenses that go along with leaving home for college. You can then transfer to the final University where you want to get your degree (in some instances, it is actually easier to get into a University as a transfer student). Your final degree will have the name of that university on it and nobody will care that you went to the community college to knock out the first two years of basic courses.

Don't pay someone to do a job for you if you have the skill to do it yourself or you can teach yourself.

YouTube® videos are an excellent resource. I have learned to do basic plumbing, replace the screen on my cell phone, change brake pads, replace a radiator, etc. etc. Take the time to look up a repair before you pay someone else. I have been surprised how easy it is to repair stuff. I also found that I can get just about any tool or replacement item from the internet. Try it, you just might save you a ton of money and give yourself a boost in confidence.

Put your savings in a place that is difficult to reach

By this I mean that it should literally be in a place that is inconvenient for you to get to it. I would suggest that you keep your savings in a separate Credit Union or Bank that is not close to where you live. Also, do not take out any ATM or Bank Cards that can access those funds. In this way, you know that you will only "raid" these savings in an emergency.

Create a 50/50 savings plan for your children

One of the best things we did was create a 50/50 savings plan for our children. What this means is that if one of our children wanted to buy something big and we approved of the purchase then we would go in 50/50 with them. This way they would have "skin in the game" and we would find out real quick if this was important to them or not. As an example, my son wanted a $500 guitar. He did not have $500 or even $100 at the time. So we set up the savings plan. As he saved money, we would match it dollar for dollar until he had enough for the guitar. It is a great plan that teaches the kids to save, but also allows you to bless them as they save. They learn the responsibility of saving and also determine if the really "want" the item they are saving for. Many times once they have all the money saved they realize the item they wanted is really not worth it after all.

Plant a garden if you have extra yard or land

Even a small garden can save you money. We love planting tomatoes and cucumbers. They are easy to grow and don't take up much room in the yard. It is also a fun activity to teach your children.

Have an energy audit done on your house

Many utility companies will do this for low/no cost and you can see where to save money on your heating and air

Set your thermostats to the most economical level

Generally this means 68 degrees in the winter when you are home and 78 degrees in the summer when you are home. Purchase a programmable thermostat so that you can set different temperatures when you are away from your home. There is no use in heating and cooling an empty house. If you can stand it in the winter, you can even turn down the thermostat a few more degrees and save even more (just put on an extra layer of clothing).

Set up your saving to be automatic

Have the money for saving taken out of your paycheck automatically and you will never miss is it and you will learn to live on less.

Get generic prescription drug whenever possible

Ask your doctor if a generic is available. If not, see how much your current drug costs and if it is too expensive, then ask if there is a reasonable substitute that might be less expensive.

I know my Bride needed some medication that did not have a generic available yet and the cost was $98.00 per bottle. We asked for an alternative and found one for $2.00 per bottle. It is worth asking.

Shop around for expensive dental work

When my kids needed braces, we went to all of our friends and got recommendations for good Orthodontists. We had 5 really good recommendations. We then compared this list with the ones covered by our insurance and found that three were a match. We went to all three and asked them for a quote and ended up saving over $1,500!! That is real money.

Put all your loose change in one place

You will be amazed at how much money you will have at the end of the year. We belong to a Credit Union that lets us use their coin counting machine for free.

Use your local library for entertainment

You will be amazed at the stuff they have at the library these days and it is free! In the age of the internet, many people have forgotten about their local library.

Make your own laundry detergent

I know this sounds crazy, but it works! It is really easy to do, and you save a ton of money. There are plenty of recipes on the internet to follow and I promise you will save big bucks. It is also a fun activity to do with the kids. This is something my daughter and I do every 90 to 120 day.

Cancel your cell phone contract and get a monthly plan

We use a plan from Walmart that is $45 per month for an iPhone. It gives us all the data, text and talk we need. Our coverage is great and we save a ton of money. Buy a used cell phone and save more.

Switch to CFL or LED lighting

Yes these types of bulbs are more expensive, but they last much longer and save money in the long run. If money is tight, then just slowly change out your bulbs as they go out.

Cancel those newspaper and magazine subscriptions

You can read all the news you want for free on the internet You can also go to the library if you really want to read that magazine or newspaper.

Do not buy on impulse

If you really think you need it, then wait 24 - 48 hours before you buy it and then see if you still need it. Waiting will save you money.

Borrowing Money/Debt

The only thing I recommend borrowing money for is a house. Other than that, pay cash. This is what we have done and it is a sacrifice, but well worth it in the long run.

One of the key issues that couples fight over is money and debt. You can eliminate a lot of headache and heartache by not going into debt.

Avoid debt at all cost! Pay cash or cash flow

Don't buy what you can't pay for in full. Enough said!

Never borrow money for college!!!!!

I am convinced that one of the greatest gifts is helping our children graduate from college without debt. It can be done. It is not always easy, but it is better than the alternative - saddling our children with unsustainable student loan debt.

Consider this; you can almost never get rid of student loan debt except to pay it off. It cannot be discharged in bankruptcy, and in some instances if you co-sign, even if your child dies, you could be liable for the debt. We read a story about this the other day on the web. A young lady had $100k+ student loan debt and died. Because her parents co-signed they must now pay off this debt.

Start saving now for college. It is a sacrifice that has long term benefits.

Never borrow money for a depreciating asset (cars, boats, trucks, snow mobiles, trailers, etc).

If you really want those things (listed above), then save your money and pay cash. Drive a reliable used car and then just rent the other stuff as you need it. If you drive an older car, it is a good idea to have AAA coverage of some other type of road service in case of breakdowns.

Be aligned with your spouse on not borrowing money!

This plan will only work if both of you are on the same page. You both need to be completely committed to not being in debt or borrowing money.

No debt - no credit cards, no charge accounts!

Do you see a theme here? This means no credit cards! Get a debit card linked to your checking and savings account. This way you can never spend more than you make.

Don't pay interest - you should be earning interest! This is a side benefit of not having any debt. Instead of you paying interest to a credit card company you can earn interest in money you have invested.

Do not borrow money to buy things you do not need, to impress people you do not know

Keeping up with the Jones is a dangerous game to get into. While you might think your friends and family have lots of "toys" and pretty things, consider that most of them are probably swimming in debt themselves as they try to impress others.

Not borrowing today, sets you up for future success

I know it is hard for you to see 25-30 years down the road and the impact of your decisions. I have walked this path and I can tell you that it is worth the journey of not being in debt and beholden to others. It is a blessing to look around at your possessions and know you own them all and not having the stress of payments.

If you have debt, then make it your goal to pay it off quickly

If you already have some credit card or student loan debt, then just buckle down, cut your expenses, take an extra job and do whatever it takes to get yourself free from this debt. You will be so proud of yourself and I know you will enjoy your new found financial freedom. I recommend you use a resource like Dave Ramsey (daveramsey.com) to learn how to effectively eliminate debt.

Retirement

Save money for retirement

Yes I know this sounds kind of basic, but you would not believe how few people do not plan for or save for retirement. 15% to 20% of your gross income is a good starting place, but at a minimum, take advantage of your companies 401k savings match or if you are self-employed the 403b plan.

It is never too early to start saving for retirement

Ideally you want to start saving for retirement as soon as you start your first real job. Do not hesitate and do not wait. The time value of money and the magic of compounding interest are your best retirement friends. It will seem small at first but I can testify that it is very real! The small savings from my first 5 years of work is worth well over six figures. This is from a small salary base in the 1980's. I am now much closer to retirement and very glad I saved money from the very first pay check.

It is never too late to start saving for retirement

Ok. If you are 65 and have not started saving for retirement, then it may be too late for you. However, some of you may not have had the opportunity to start saving early for retirement. Start today. It is better to start now and have a little saved than nothing at all.

Learn about all the different savings options available to you

You should be a student of retirement and start your education early. You should get to know retirement terminology like:

- 401K
- SIMPLE IRA
- Traditional IRA
- Roth IRA
- 403B
- SEP IRA's

Do not count on Social Security or the Government for your retirement.

I am in my mid-50's as I am writing this book and I have **ZERO** confidence in Social Security being available for myself or for my children.   As of 2015 - Social Security is headed for insolvency by 2034.   That is 19 years from now.

I have **ZERO** confidence in the government's ability to take care of me in my old age.   This is something you must do and secure for yourself.   You cannot and should not depend on others for this responsibility.

Believe in the power of Compounding Interest over time

If we assume two different people each earn the same 7% return on their investment - the only difference is the amount of time they have for that money to accrue.

Here is an example of the power of compounding interest:

Person A - saved $1,000 per month from the time he turned 25 until he turned 35. Then he stopped saving but left his money in his investment account until he retired at age 65.

Person B - did not start saving until age 35. They put away the same $1,000 per month from their 35th birthday until they turned 45.   They left the balance in their investment account just like person A until age 65.

They each saved the same amount — $120,000 — over a 10 year period.

By age 65 the balances were dramatically different. Person A would have about $ 1,440,000 and Person B would have about $735,000.   The only difference is the amount of time!   Start saving now!

Do not ever touch your retirement saving

Do not touch this money until retirement.   You might think of taking a loan against the money. Don't do it. You might think of withdrawing early. Don't do it (there is a 10% penalty and you have to pay taxes). The money is for retirement only. Have that mindset going in when you start saving for retirement.

Spending

Have a monthly/weekly budget

You have to know where your money is going; the best way to account for the money is to have a budget for all of your expenses. If you are married, then you need to make sure that you and your spouse are completely aligned to the budget and how you will spend your money.

Never spend money before you have it.

This means no credit cards or debt. This is a common theme in this chapter.

Garage/Yard sales are an incredible way to find good bargains (and work on your negotiating skills).

This can also be a lot of fun. When my children were younger, we would take them out and find some "new" toys, games or books. A very inexpensive date!

Cut the cord and stop spending money on cable or satellite TV.

According to the FCC the average American spends about $65 each month on cable TV. That works out to $780 per year or $31,200 over 40 years! Ouch!!! With the ability to stream digital TV for free with an antenna this seems crazy to me. There is also so much free content on the web these days, that the need to pay to watch TV is a true luxury that few can justify. We have NEVER paid to watch TV!

Thrift stores are an excellent place to save money.

We probably purchase about 90% of our clothing at the thrift store. We have also found great pieces of furniture and other household goods. If you are a cloths snob, get over yourself and look for the name brand bargains! Nobody will know the clothes are from the thrift store unless you tell them.

Pay your bills on time.

If you want to avoid late charges or re-connect fees - then make paying all of your bills on time a top priority. It is also the right thing to do.

Do not go grocery shopping when you are hungry

This one may seem silly, but it is true! Also, if you can avoid shopping with you kids that will also save money. They have a cute but annoying way of asking for stuff they do not need and we don't have the ability to say no to.

When you go to the grocery store - have a list and stick to it!

It is too easy to get sucked into buying stuff you do not need. Have a good list and just purchase those items

The following statements all speak for themselves.

- Spend less than you earn
- Keep life simple and live within your means
- Do not try to keep up with the Jones

Renting is a good way to enjoy something without a long term commitment.

If you don't live on the water, don't buy a boat. It is cheaper to rent one when you need it. The same thing goes for an RV. If you are not fully retired and living in the RV, then just rent it when you need it.

Try to never buy new text books for college

It is much easier to rent them, buy them used or better yet borrow from a friend who took the class before you. I know from hard experience with myself and kids that you can save a lot of money this way.

Leave your wallet in the car

Only take the cash you need for the items you are looking for. You want to make it very inconvenient for yourself to spend money. Of course, this assumes that you followed the original advice and got rid of your credit cards and have switched to cash.

Do not buy something new, especially if it is a depreciating asset (like a car).

Learn to buy good used items. Examples:
- ✓ Toys
- ✓ Cloths
- ✓ Just about anything with an engine
- ✓ Furniture
- ✓ DVD/VHS movies
- ✓ Electronics
- ✓ Books

These days there really is not any reason to buy new unless you absolutely just want to spend the money. With tools on the web like Ebay and Amazon, you can find plenty of the items that you want used, and many sites offer guarantees on these items.

When you go grocery shopping, buy the store brands and or use coupons.

 If you want to save even more money, then buy the store private label brands. They are almost always cheaper and the quality is quite good. Always calculate the ounces or servings to compare with national brands to see if you are really saving money.   Sometimes when you use a coupon and sale price you can get national brands cheaper.

Have a freezer and buy in bulk when things are on sale.

 If you have room for and can afford an additional freezer, then this is an excellent way to stock up and save money.   Many times you can find meat, fish, bread, cheese and vegetables on sale.   All of these things keep well in the freezer.

Learn to negotiate

Some might say haggle, but whatever you call it, don't pay the asking price when you might get it cheaper. Offer cash and a lower price and many times people will take the immediate cash offer.   Always ask for a discount whether it is service product or a tangible item.

Get the highest insurance deductible you can on all your assets.

This will save you considerable money each month.   The key to this strategy is to have the emergency saving available in case disaster strikes.   You can raise the deductible on your house to $5,000 and your premium will shrink! However, you better have $5,000 in emergency saving.

You will read later that I recommend buying good older used cars. One of the biggest savings is that I do not need to purchase replacement coverage (which is really expensive).   I just need to have enough money in savings to purchase another used vehicle in case my car is totaled (by me).

Buy term life insurance!

Term Life Insurance offers the most coverage for the least cost. It is also the easiest to understand.   I know this will make many insurance agents unhappy, but I am not worried about making them happy, I am worried about you saving money.   The common wisdom is to get life insurance 10x your salary. Therefore, if you make $100,000 per year, then you will need $1,000,000 in term life insurance. The whole point of life insurance is to offer protection for your family in case of your death and to replace you income. It is not an investment vehicle or opportunity to make money.

Buy an umbrella insurance policy

This is a type of insurance that covers you in excess of the liability limits of your other insurance policies. Below is a better definition:

Umbrella insurance is extra liability insurance. It is designed to help protect you from major claims and lawsuits and as a result it helps protect your assets and your future.

For me, this is as much about peace of mind as anything else.   I see this as a prudent financial investment.

Shop around every 2-3 years to compare insurance rates

I have found that staying with one insurance provider generally leads to complacency on their part and rates tend to creep up and up. By shopping around and comparing rates, I can keep my insurance company honest and also pay the lowest premiums.

Wait for the sales before you buy anything

This can be true at a major retailer or even at a thrift store. One of the thrift stores we shop has a different "color" they use each week to offer additional discounts up to 50% off. While it does not sound like much, it adds up over time. We also get "free" money in the form of store coupons from a particular retailer. There are no strings attached and it is usually $10.00. We then go to this retailer and look for something that cost $10.00 or less. Then it is truly free.

Buy the fresh food when it is in season

If you buy fresh blue berries in the off season, they can be very expensive. If you only purchase them when they are in season, they can be very reasonable. This can be true for most fresh food. Below is an example of some items and when to buy and save the most money:

Apples	August - November
Blue Berries	May - August
Carrots	Year Round
Cherries	April - July
Corn	June - November
Grapes	July - November
Green Beans	June - October
Lemons	Year Round
Lettuce	Year Round
Oranges	Year Round
Peaches	May - October
Potatoes	June - August
Strawberries	March - November
Sweet Potatoes	September - December
Tree Nuts	September - November
Tomatoes	June - November

__Investing__

Always take advantage of your 401K match!

If your company has a 401K plan - take full advantage at the earliest possible date. Invest early and often.

Maximize your 401K and or Roth Accounts

Not only should you take advantage of your companies 401K, you should also max out your contributions to the legal limit. If you invest in a Roth account, take advantage of that as well.

Invest early and often in no-load mutual funds

If you have the ability to invest outside of your company's 401K plan, then look into these types of funds. You should look at mutual fund companies like Vanguard, Fidelity and T.Rowe Price as options to consider. (There are a ton of mutual fund companies out there to choose from and I have only listed three. You should do your own research on which company offers you the best investment and cost options to meet your needs).

A no load mutual fund is a fund that does not charge you an up-front fee or back end fees to invest in that fund.

This is a great way to build wealth and prepare for retirement.

Land is a real asset that never has zero value

While land and property are not very liquid assets (meaning that you cannot generally sell them quickly), they do tend to be assets that hold their value over the long run. The key is buying land and property when it is very cheap and holding onto it. Remember that outside of your primary home, you should not be borrowing money. If you don't have the cash to buy additional land and property then skip it.

Do not invest in anything that you cannot explain to a 6th grader!

If you don't understand it, then don't invest in it.

A home is an asset that appreciates in value over the long haul.

Yes, there can be ups and downs in the real estate market, but a home is generally a good investment and the only investment that I would recommend you borrow money to purchase.   You should have a minimum of 20% down (25%-30% is better) and you should be able to afford a 15 year fixed rate loan.   If you cannot meet those parameters, then rent until you can!

One of the reasons for the 20% down payment is to avoid PMI insurance. PMI insurance is insurance that the mortgage company forces you to buy to protect **them** in case you fail to pay your mortgage.   It is very expensive and you want to avoid paying this at all costs.

Own very little stock in the company you work for

It is a sad tale that is told again and again of people who had their entire retirement in company stock and the company declined, sold or went out of business and they lost their entire nest egg. See next advice

Do not put all your eggs in one basket

You should have a diversified portfolio of assets such as: no-load mutual funds, cash, bonds, real estate etc.   You have to consider how much risk you can tolerate, and spread your assets accordingly. There are many theories and advice on how to balance your assets as there are people. You should seek advice from someone who has successfully navigated these waters and has no vested interest in the outcome - other than to see you do well.

I have an older gentleman who has been a financial mentor of mine. I go to him often to seek advice on how to best manage my portfolio. He is just an older, wiser and very successful man who is a friend and has my best interest in mind.

Do not take unsolicited financial advice from someone who calls you or sends you an e-mail, text or note on Facebook.

You should approach financial professionals, not the other way around.   My advice - RUN!!

Invest in your financial knowledge and education

You need to invest some time and money by buying some books or attending financial seminars - such as those by Dave Ramsey.   He has excellent advice about budgeting, investing and getting out of debt and staying out of debt.

This will pay dividends all the years of your life (pun intended).   Seek wise counsel for others who you know, trust and respect.

Seek advice from a fee based financial planner

This is a person who will charge you a flat fee for advice and will not try to sell you things you do not need.   If the financial planner is not fee based, then they are working on commission and could try to sell you things that are good for them (because of high fees) and not good for you.

Giving

Be generous with you time, talents and treasures - especially with your family first

They say that charity begins at home. Make sure that you are taking care of your family first and then reach out to your friends and neighbors. When you give, give generously, with a glad heart and smile on your face. I have never regretted anything I ever gave away.

Give a minimum of 10% of your income and time to charity

The only antidote to greed is to be a giver! As a Christian we are called to give a 10% tithe to the church. I will tell you that this is the starting place and certainly not the ending place for giving.

The side benefit is that this is also a very good tax write-off (but this should not be the reason for giving).

Be a volunteer.

There is nothing stronger than the heart of a volunteer. Share your time with others and give back to your church, neighborhood and community.

Support those go on mission trips to share the gospel

I have had the opportunity to go on many missions trips around the world and this was only possible by the faithful giving of those supported these trips.

I also learned a valuable lesson from one of my Sunday-School teachers many years ago. He was an excellent example of someone who committed to support any and all people who sent him support letters. At times this tested his faith and financial resources, but he always gave. As a family we have made this same commitment and I cannot begin to tell you what a blessing this has been in our lives. We have had the opportunity to be the answer to many prayer requests and I can honestly say that it is a real honor and privilege to be God's instrument to answer a prayer request.

Other Money Advice

- Money is only a tool - it is neither good nor bad.   Treat it as a tool and don't worship it.

- There is no such thing as get rich quick; it takes hard work and discipline

- If you have rental property, always secure a large deposit (a month or two of rent) and do not return it without a complete and thorough inspection.   Never allow pets! Pets are a disaster for rental property.

- Do not be penny wise and pound foolish

- Never lend money to others (especially family) but be quick to offer assistance and help

- Do not let your Jay Bird eyes; overload your Humming bird stomach

- It's not how much you make; it's what you do with what you make.

- A fool and his money are soon parted.

- A penny saved is a penny earned.

- Charity begins at home

Quotes on Money

"Rich people have small TVs and big libraries, and poor people have small libraries and big TVs." **Zig Ziglar**

"Compound interest is the eighth wonder of the world. He who understands it, earns it ... he who doesn't ... pays it."
Albert Einstein

"Compound interest is the most powerful force in the universe."
Albert Einstein

"Compound interest is the greatest mathematical discovery of all time." **Albert Einstein**

"Money never made a man happy yet, nor will it. The more a man has, the more he wants. Instead of filling a vacuum, it makes one."
Ben Franklin

"Too many people spend money they earned, to buy things they don't want, to impress people that they don't like". **Will Rogers**

"Financial peace isn't the acquisition of stuff. It's learning to live on less than you make, so you can give money back and have money to invest. You can't win until you do this." **Dave Ramsey**

"Beware of little expenses. A small leak will sink a great ship."
Ben Franklin

"A wise person should have money in their head, but not in their heart." **Jonathan Swift**

"He that is of the opinion money will do everything may well be suspected of doing everything for money." **Ben Franklin**

"We make a living by what we get, but we make a life by what we give." **Winston Churchill**

"Early to bed and early to rise, makes a man healthy, wealthy and wise" **Ben Franklin**

"You must gain control over your money or the lack of it will forever control you." **Dave Ramsey**

"Wealth is the parent of luxury and indolence, and poverty of meanness and viciousness, and both of discontent." **Plato**

"Never spend your money before you have earned it."
Thomas Jefferson

"Greed is not a financial issue. It's a heart issue." **Andy Stanley**

"Wealth consists not in having great possessions, but in having few wants." **Epictetus**

"Money is only a tool. It will take you wherever you wish, but it will not replace you as the driver." **Ayn Rand**

"The real measure of your wealth is how much you'd be worth if you lost all your money." **Anonymous**

"Money is a terrible master but an excellent servant". **P.T. Barnum**

"Before you speak, listen. Before you write, think. Before you spend, earn. Before you invest, investigate. Before you criticize, wait. Before you pray, forgive. Before you quit, try. Before you retire, save. Before you die, give." **William A. Ward**

"No wealth can ever make a bad man at peace with himself." **Plato**

"If you know how to spend less than you get, you have the philosopher's stone." **Ben Franklin**

"When prosperity comes, do not use all of it". **Confucius**

.

Bible Verses on Money

Deuteronomy 8:18
But you shall remember the Lord your God, for it is He who is giving you power to make wealth, that He may confirm His covenant which He swore to your fathers, as it is this day.

Proverbs 3:9
Honor the Lord from your wealth, And from the first of all your produce

1 Timothy 6:10
For the love of money is a root of all sorts of evil, and some by longing for it have wandered away from the faith and pierced themselves with many griefs.

Ecclesiastes 5:10
He who loves money will not be satisfied with money, nor he who loves abundance with its income. This too is vanity.

Matthew 6:24
No one can serve two masters; for either he will hate the one and love the other, or he will be devoted to one and despise the other. You cannot serve God and wealth.

Proverbs 11:15
He who is guarantor for a stranger will surely suffer for it, But he who hates being a guarantor is secure.

Malachi 3:10
Bring the whole tithe into the storehouse, so that there may be food in My house, and test Me now in this," says the Lord of hosts, "if I will not open for you the windows of heaven and pour out for you a blessing until it overflows.

Matthew 6:21
For where your treasure is, there your heart will be also.

Psalm 37:16-17
Better is the little of the righteous, Than the abundance of many wicked. For the arms of the wicked will be broken, But the Lord sustains the righteous.

Proverbs 13:11
Wealth obtained by fraud dwindles,
But the one who gathers by labor increases it.

Hebrews 13:5
Make sure that your character is free from the love of money,
being content with what you have;
for He Himself has said, "I will never desert you, nor will I ever forsake you,"

Luke 3:14
Some soldiers were questioning him (Jesus), saying, "And what about us,
what shall we do?" And he said to them, "Do not take money from anyone by
force, or accuse anyone falsely, and be content with your wages."

1 Timothy 6:17-19
Instruct those who are rich in this present world not to be conceited or to fix
their hope on the uncertainty of riches, but on God, who richly supplies us
with all things to enjoy. Instruct them to do good, to be rich in good works, to
be generous and ready to share, storing up for themselves the treasure of a
good foundation for the future, so that they may take hold of that which is life
indeed.

Deuteronomy 15:7
If there is a poor man with you, one of your brothers, in any of your towns in
your land which the Lord your God is giving you, you shall not harden your
heart, nor close your hand from your poor brother;

Proverbs 10:4
Poor is he who works with a negligent hand, But the hand of the diligent
makes rich.

Ecclesiastes 7:12
For wisdom is protection just as money is protection, but the advantage of
knowledge is that wisdom preserves the lives of its possessors.

Matthew 16:26
For what will it profit a man if he gains the whole world and forfeits his soul?
Or what will a man give in exchange for his soul?

1 Timothy 5:8
But if anyone does not provide for his own, and especially for those of his
household, he has denied the faith and is worse than an unbeliever.

Matthew 5:23-24

Therefore if you are presenting your offering at the altar, and there remember that your brother has something against you, leave your offering there before the altar and go; first be reconciled to your brother, and then come and present your offering.

Proverbs 23:5

When you set your eyes on it, it is gone.
For wealth certainly makes itself wings
Like an eagle that flies toward the heavens.

Proverbs 23:4

Do not weary yourself to gain wealth,
Cease from your [a]consideration of it.

Proverbs 13:22

A good man leaves an inheritance to his children's children,
And the wealth of the sinner is stored up for the righteous.

Proverbs 13:7

There is one who pretends to be rich but has nothing;
Another pretends to be poor, but has great wealth.

Work

Work is something we can never get away from. We will work from our young age until our old age. Work does not always mean a "job" that pays money. We have work to do at home, church, community, and school to just name a few places. However, most of the context in this chapter refers to work as a "job" where we do get paid a wage.

The best boss you will ever have is yourself

If you can be self-employed and work for yourself, then you will almost always be better off in the long run. Working for someone else means their rules, regulations and putting up with their personality and foibles.

Treat those below you at work with as much respect as those above you (same thing for those at the same level)

Not only is this the kind and right thing to do, you never know who is going to be the next boss. I have had plenty of younger co-workers who passed me along the way and are now in higher positions of authority.

There is no room for arrogance at work

Humility is a much better work partner. Try to get along with everyone as much as possible.

Surround yourself with people smarter and wiser than you

This is tough, because it means you have to swallow your pride and admit there are people smarter than yourself. However, if you can pull this off, then the team that you create can get so much more done than you could have done alone.

You do not know it all, so do not be a "know it all"

See the point before! In addition, nobody likes a know it all.

Praise in public, criticize in private

When you have people reporting to you, it is important to share praise and recognition publicly. If you need to correct or criticize, then do this in private. This works at home as well.

Good news should travel fast, but bad news should travel faster

One of my early bosses told me this and it is so true. It is much better to tell the bad news as quickly as possible. Nobody likes bad surprises.

There is no substitute for hard work

No further comment needed!

It takes 10,000 hours to master a skill

This comes from the book "Outliers" by Malcom Gladwell.   The basic premise is that it is only through hard work and commitment that you can become an expert.   When you think about it, 10,000 hours would equate to 4 years of working 40 hours per week at a skill.

It is ok to start at the bottom and work your way up

To many young people these days seem to come to work with a sense of entitlement.   Unless your relatives own the company, you will probably start near the bottom.   Embrace the challenge and learn as much as possible.

Remember who signs your paycheck - that is who you work for!

Sometimes in your career, you will have multiple people who think they are your boss. It is the person who signs the paycheck and does the annual performance appraisal who is your boss. That does not mean you can ignore these other people, it just means you have to be focused on meeting the needs of your own manager first.

The boss's priorities are your priorities!

Stay within these parameters and life usually goes better at work.

Nobody ever said "I wish I had spent more time at work"

This is all about knowing where your real priorities lie.   Go home to your family and friends and spend time with them.   The work will always be there.   Do not be one of those pitiful people who make their job their life and sacrifice their family at the altar of their career.

It is called work for a reason

It is supposed to be hard, and sometimes boring and methodical.   It will never always be fun and a joy.   That is why you are a professional and they pay you a salary.   Push through those tough times and get the job done. Continue to show up and do the work.

Everybody reports to somebody

In other words, everybody has a boss.   A one star general reports to a three star general.

You are a leader, whether you believe it or not

Whether your title or position at work designates you as leader, you are already one.   Do not believe for one second that you are not a leader.   Act like a leader, make tough choices and decisions and offer you opinion.

You are always on stage, never forget that someone is always watching

What I mean by this is that you can never let your guard down at work and most especially at events outside of work. People are constantly watching you to see how you will act and react. That is why it is so important for you to be yourself and not to pretend you are something you are not.   Be consistent at work and away from work.

Dress for success

You should know what the dress code is for you company. Some are formal, some are casual. Remember that everything communicates. How you choose to dress is an expression of who you are. Even if it is not important to you, it very well may be important to your boss and others you report to. I have had more than one boss who was a stickler for dress codes. I have had other managers who did not care one way or the other. Know your environment and the image you want to project. Generally speaking - sloppy, ill-fitting and mismatched is not a fashion statement; it is a recipe for disaster.

Lead, follow or get out of the way

Not much else to say here. If you stand in the middle of the road, you will get run over.

Measure twice cut once

Something my grandfather taught me as a young boy. Before we would cut a piece of wood, we would always measure it twice to make sure it was right. If you got the cut wrong, then the piece of wood would be ruined and you would have wasted time and money. What this speaks to is attention to detail.

Also, never assume a piece of wood is the length advertised! I was once cutting some boards for a community project and we needed an 8ft board. We had purchased all the lumber in 8ft lengths so I just sent the board with the team without measuring it. They came back later and had me cut 1 1/2 inches from the board. It was longer than advertised. I wasted their time and energy by not measuring.

Never use a new razor before a date or job interview

Unless you want to look like your face just got attacked by zombies it is best not to use a new razor before that job interview. I have made this mistake and left nicks all over my face. Not a good first impression.

Shine your shoes, trim your nails, and shave closely

First impressions are very important and can create lasting impressions. If you have a beard or mustache be sure to neatly trim it.

You cannot have it all

There are always sacrifices that need to be made with either your job or family commitments.   I have been working for 30+ years and I have never met anyone who "has it all" including me.

You can and should work very hard to balance your work and personal life, but this is really hard and will require constant vigilance on your part.   It is too easy to lean one way or the other.

If you lean too hard into work, then you sacrifice your family. If you lean too hard into family, you might lose your job.   It is a constant balancing act.   I have found in my job there are "seasons" where I have to lean into the work.   However, I try very hard to not make those "seasons" last all year long.

From my point of view, this comes down to priorities and where you ultimately want to spend your time. I would argue that if you are consistently working 50+ hours per week that it would be very challenging to "have it all".

I will say that every moment with your family is precious and you should cherish that time.

If you are not part of the solution, you are part of the problem

Decide if you want to be part of the team and to contribute to solving issues. Do not bring up problems without offering a solution. Anybody can point out a problem.

Nobody is going to care as much about your career and job as you do

It is up to you to work on your career development, knowledge and network.   A boss or manager can create a better atmosphere, but you have to do the work.

Volunteer for the hard and dirty tasks

This is as much a leadership function as it is teamwork function.   You can almost never go wrong with this attitude.

It is up to you to create "work/life" balance

Nobody can do this for you. You have to do this yourself. Remember that a job will bleed you dry if you let it. Most people desire to have some sort of balance in their life, but they are afraid to step out and do the right thing. Everybody else is working like a dog and sacrificing their family, so you think you should as well. Don't do it. Decide to be different. I can promise you that when you walk away from work that last day, nobody will miss you very long,. But if you miss all of the important events in your family's life they will always remember you not being there. Remember that you cannot redeem a single day. Once a day is done, it is done.

I was walking down the hallway with a former manager of mine and he told me that he had missed almost every game his daughter had played that season. I asked him about an upcoming meeting the next week and his immediate response was "I would not miss that meeting for the world". WOW! He would not miss the meeting, but was willing to miss seeing his daughter compete. I was very disappointed in the manager and clearly this is not someone that I want to emulate. The sad part of this is that he only has the one daughter and that daughter is going to be grown and gone very quickly. This manager is a "rising star" in the company and I am sure he will go far, but I wonder if he will ever consider the cost before it is too late?

Who you work for (meaning who your boss is), is just as or even more important than the work itself

I have had great jobs with a terrible manager and terrible jobs with a great manager. I have also had a great jobs with a great manager. What I have found is that a great manager is always the difference and can make even a bad job feel good. Be very careful who you work for. If you work for a tyrant, move on!

Learn to network and know people across different job functions.

This will help you better understand your job and how it fits within the context of the entire company. It will also expand your knowledge base and make you a more valuable asset to the company. You will also be exposed to new jobs that you might enjoy.

You only have to be 1% better than everybody else to shine

You do not have to be 100% better than everyone else. You only have to outperform them by a little bit to be a shining star. Always strive to give you best effort each day with each task you are assigned.

Deliver more than you are asked for.

Keep a toothbrush at work

Not only is this good for dental hygiene, but your team mates will appreciate it as well.

Mints and gum are a good thing to keep with you or at your desk

This is not only for yourself, but for your guests as well. It can be a nice opening gesture to someone who comes to your work space.

Fewer PowerPoint slides are always better than more.

Always strive to make your presentations shorter and more to the point. Less is more! It is much more difficult to put together a short presentation than a long presentation. Remember that the Gettysburg address was delivered in less than 2 minutes and the speaker before had given a speech that lasted almost 2 hours. Who was that first speaker? Exactly! Nobody remembers the long address, only what President Lincoln said in brevity. BTW it was Secretary of State Edward Everett who delivered the speech before Lincoln.

Return - email, voicemail, text, instant message, phone call etc. promptly!

Nobody likes to be ignored or forgotten. A good general rule of thumb is to respond within 24 hours. However, I would suggest that if possible you should try to respond by the end of the day, even if your note is just an acknowledgment that you are working on the issue.

The only caveat to this advice is to recognize that in some jobs and companies, things can be very time sensitive, so responding within the hour might be more appropriate. Either way, you should know the dynamics of response within you company.

However, if you are angry, frustrated or mad, do not reply to a message promptly!

It is best to write your initial reply and then put it in the draft folder and think about it a couple of hours or even over night if possible. You should also consider seeking out advice from someone who can offer an objective opinion before you reply.

Just the other night I received an e-mail that frustrated me greatly. I wanted to lash out and say something harmful. I actually wrote four e-mail messages that I never sent (thankfully) and slept on the issue. The next morning, it did not seem quite as dire as I thought and I had a clearer mind and frame of reference. Very glad I did not hit the send button.

If you do not know the answer, then at least try to help find the answer

Do not just tell someone you do not know, go the extra distance and try to help find someone who can help.

Show up early for meetings (you usually get a better seat)

It is almost never good to show up late to meetings. Do not make it a habit showing up late. I had one manager who had the following mantra:

"Early is on-time and on-time is late". He was serious about this!!

It's ok to ask for help

You do not know everything, and I can promise you this, as you rise in your company you will have to rely more and more on subject matter experts to answer questions. Asking for help is a sign of maturity.

No job is worth sacrificing your integrity

Walk away from any job that requires you to sacrifice your integrity. Remember, your integrity can never be taken from you; you can only give it away.

There will always be "slackers" in every work environment

Avoid them at all costs. I have never been on a team of all super stars. There is usually someone who wants to hide in the shadows and ride the coattails of the team. These slackers are a drag on the team and a waste of time and energy.

Beware of the whiner

Every work place has this type of person. They are like the plague, deadly and completely unhelpful. We all have occasional complaints and problems, but some people seem to thrive on whining and bringing everybody else down. RUN away from the whiner!!

In a meeting, write down your questions before you ask them

This will help you gather your thoughts before you ask a question. Many times your question will be answered if you wait just a little longer.

Do not use your computer, pad, or phone when someone else is presenting

Not only is this rude, but you will probably miss some important information. Choose to be the person in the meeting who is paying attention. Also, even if you are taking notes on your computer, it can appear that your are distracted or disinterested.

Have a robust password

You want a password that is difficult for others but easy for you. Seems like common sense these days, but this is very important to do. If possible, use a combination of Upper and Lower case letter as well as special symbols. If you can make your password 8-12 characters long, this will help as well (longer is better of course). Change your password often (either weekly or monthly).

Do not goof off on the job - it is a good way to get fired

This means not playing games on your phone or computer, no sleeping on the job and no wasting time endlessly surfing the web. You will get caught. It is only a matter of time.

Work hard at company community events

If your company is participating in a community event (like building a house for Habitat for Humanity), then make sure you are one of the hardest workers and willing to do the dirty and hard tasks. You can always tell a lot about a person at these type of events. Many come to be "seen", but do not actually want to do any work. I promise you that people will notice who is working and who is slacking off.

Do not date someone you work with

There are several reasons for this advice.

1. There is the real potential for conflict of interest and favoritism

2. If you do break up it **WILL** be weird at work. You have to continue to see this person every day.

Use - "Unless Directed Otherwise"

I learned this from a book I read call Rouge Warrior. Basically, sometimes you just need to get stuff done and others are a road block because they will not make a decision. You can present them with a choice and conclude with the following statement: *"Unless Directed Otherwise -I will be making the following decisions"*. This forces the issue one way or the other. You will either move forward with your decision or you will get an answer from them. It can be a bit risky and you should proceed with caution. It can also be very effective.

Sometimes at work it is better to ask forgiveness then permission

This goes along with the advice above. There are times when you need to move a project along and you cannot get permission or the process and procedures in place make it very difficult. You have to be very careful how you use this advice though. Understand the risks, because if you make a huge error you could lose your job!

Trust but verify

This was a saying that Ronald Regan used when dealing with USSR. I have found it very useful with both my family as well as business situations. This is especially useful with strangers.

Unless you are independently wealthy or have a family business - plan to go to College, Trade School or the Military

There are basically three choices available to most people who do not have wealth or a family business.

College - a four year degree from an accredited university is still one of the best paths to a good job. The key is to major in a subject where there are actual jobs. If you major in Medieval History, do not be surprised if you are working fast food after college.   Here are some specific degree (in no order and not comprehensive) - Engineer, Accountant, Physical Therapist, Nurse, Teacher, etc.

Associates Degree/Junior College - there are a ton of great jobs you can get without a four year degree. An associate's degree opens a lot of doors to jobs that pay very well.

Trade School - not everyone needs, wants or desires to go to college. Trade school is an excellent route to getting a good job and career. Most people do not realize to become a licensed plumber or electrician you need four years of study and apprenticeship.   There are a ton of good career options where you usually get to work with your hands and mind.

Military - while not for everyone it is an honorable profession where you learn leadership and teamwork as well as real skills that are transferable to life outside of the military.

The alternative to these three options is to become an Entrepreneur and start your own business.   As I stated at the beginning of this chapter, the best boss can ever have is yourself

Back up your computer and other devices often

You should back up your computer often.   Computers have a funny way of crashing just when you least expect it. Depending on how important your work is you may need to back up daily. Weekly is probably fine for most people and the minimum would be once per month.

Also back up your other devices! I have found it very helpful to back up the contacts on my cell phone.

You should also consider having a physical hard drive back up to supplement the "cloud" backup. I just like the idea of having the data backed up to a tangible hard drive that I can put my hands on. I don't completely trust what goes into the cloud.

Do not enter into any partnerships

The only ship that is guaranteed to sink is a partnership. It is fraught with risk and trouble. Avoid partnerships as all costs. Let me say this again for effect. **DO NOT ENTER INTO PARTNERSHIPS**.

Learn how to add value

How do you add value? You deliver more than you are asked to do. You are proactive instead of reactive. You anticipate the needs of those who you are working for. When you add value, you become "invaluable" and a welcome member of any team. You become the go to person and in time, you are given more opportunities and responsibility.

Quotes on Work

"Opportunity is missed by most people because it is dressed in overalls and looks like work." **Thomas Edison**

"I'm a great believer in luck, and I find the harder I work the more I have of it." **Thomas Jefferson**

"I have not failed. I've just found 10,000 ways that won't work." – **Thomas Edison**

"The only place where success comes before work is in the dictionary." **Vidal Sassoon**

"Well done is better than well said " **Ben Franklin**

"Beware the barrenness of a busy life." **Socrates**

"Never leave that till tomorrow which you can do today." **Ben Franklin**

"Drive thy business or it will drive thee." **Ben Franklin**

"It is well to be up before daybreak, for such habits contribute to health, wealth, and wisdom." **Aristotle**

"Life grants nothing to us mortals without hard work." **Horace**

"Diligence is the mother of good luck." **Ben Franklin**

"Necessity, who is the mother of invention." **Plato**

"The beginning is the most important part of the work." **Plato**

"Nothing ever comes to one, that is worth having, except as a result of hard work". **Booker T. Washington**

"Individual commitment to a group effort - that is what makes a team work, a company work, a society work, a civilization work."
Vince Lombardi

"The only place success comes before work is in the dictionary."
Vince Lombardi

"It is the working man who is the happy man. It is the idle man who is the miserable man." **Ben Franklin**

"Confidence is contagious and so is lack of confidence, and a customer will recognize both."   **Vince Lombardi**

"There is no substitute for hard work." **Thomas Edison**

"Whatever your life's work is, do it well. A man should do his job so well that the living, the dead, and the unborn could do it no better."
Martin Luther King, Jr.

"I do not know anyone who has got to the top without hard work. That is the recipe. It will not always get you to the top, but should get you pretty near." **Margaret Thatcher**

"Hide not your talents. They for use were made. What's a sundial in the shade." **Ben Franklin**

"Chose a job you love, and you will never have to work a day in your life." **Confucius**

"Pleasure in the job puts perfection in the work." **Aristotle**

"We are what we repeatedly do. Excellence, then, is not an act but a habit." **Aristotle**

"There is no substitute for work." **Vince Lombardi**

"Hardly any human being is capable of pursuing two professions or two arts rightly." **Plato**

"Give a man a fish, and you need him for a day. Teach a man to fish, and you feed him for a lifetime." **Chinese Proverb**

"All work and no play makes Jack a dull boy. All play and no work makes Jack a mere toy"   **Unknown**

"It is better to wear out one's shoes than one's sheets."   **Genovese**

"Implementation beats oration."   **Aesop**

"He that hath a trade, hath an estate" **Ben Franklin**

"If you have a job without any aggravations, you don't have a job." **Malcolm S. Forbes**

"What is it that you like doing? If you don't like it, get out of it, because you'll be lousy at it." **Lee Iacocca**

"Don't succumb to excuses. Go back to the job of making the corrections and forming the habits that will make your goal possible." **Vince Lombardi**

"With regard to excellence, it is not enough to know, but we must try to have and use it." **Aristotle**

"By working faithfully eight hours a day you may eventually get to be boss and work twelve hours a day." **Robert Frost**

Bible Verses on Work

Genesis 3:17
Then to Adam He said, "Because you have listened to the voice of your wife, and have eaten from the tree about which I commanded you, saying, 'You shall not eat from it'; Cursed is the ground because of you; In toil you will eat of it All the days of your life.

Colossians 3:23
Whatever you do, do your work heartily, as for the Lord rather than for men,

Proverbs 10:4
Poor is he who works with a negligent hand, But the hand of the diligent makes rich.

Proverbs 16:3
Commit your works to the Lord And your plans will be established.

Proverbs 22:29
Do you see a man skilled in his work? He will stand before kings; He will not stand before obscure men.

Proverbs 13:11
Wealth obtained by fraud dwindles, But the one who gathers by labor increases it.

Proverbs 14:23
In all labor there is profit, But mere talk leads only to poverty.

2 Corinthians 9:6
Now this I say, he who sows sparingly will also reap sparingly, and he who sows bountifully will also reap bountifully.

Galatians 6:7-9
Do not be deceived, God is not mocked; for whatever a man sows, this he will also reap. For the one who sows to his own flesh will from the flesh reap corruption, but the one who sows to the Spirit will from the Spirit reap eternal life. Let us not lose heart in doing good, for in due time we will reap if we do not grow weary.

Proverbs 6:9-11

How long will you lie down, O sluggard?
When will you arise from your sleep?
"A little sleep, a little slumber,
A little folding of the hands to rest" —
Your poverty will come in like a vagabond
And your need like an armed man.

Relationships

I thought I would start this chapter with a story about Socrates and his advice on relationships. It is an excellent example of how we should think about our friendships and how we communicate with others regarding our relationships

Socrates Advice on Relationships

In ancient Greece, Socrates was reputed to hold knowledge in high esteem. One day an acquaintance met the great philosopher and said, "Do you know what I just heard about your friend?"

"Hold on a minute," Socrates replied. "Before telling me anything I'd like you to pass a little test. It's called the Triple Filter Test."

"Triple filter?"

"That's right," Socrates continued. "Before you talk to me about my friend, it might be a good idea to take a moment and filter what you're going to say. That's why I call it the triple filter test.

The first filter is Truth. Have you made absolutely sure that what you are about to tell me is true?"

"No," the man said, "actually I just heard about it and..."

All right," said Socrates. "So you don't really know if it's true or not. Now let's try the second filter, the filter of goodness. Is what you are about to tell me about my friend something good?"

"No, on the contrary..."

"So," Socrates continued, "you want to tell me something bad about him, but you're not certain it's true. You may still pass the test though, because there's one filter left: the filter of usefulness. Is what you want to tell me about my friend going to be useful to me?"

"No, not really."

"Well," concluded Socrates, "if what you want to tell me is neither true nor good nor even useful, why tell it to me at all?"

This is why Socrates was a great philosopher & held in such high esteem.

You are well-advised to use this triple filter each time you hear loose talk about any of your near and dear friends.
The rest of the chapter is broken up into the following sections:

- Overall Advice
- Marriage
- Children
- Friends

You will spend more time, money, energy and effort on relationships than anything else in your life. Therefore it is wise to be thoughtful about how you approach these relationships.

Overall Advice

Golden rule - treat others as you want to be treated

This is a simple rule, but one that is easy to forget in our everyday life. When we are frustrated or angry is when we tend to "lash out" and not treat others as we would want to be treated. It is best to pause (if possible), take a deep breath and consider how you should treat someone else before you respond.

If you cannot keep a promise, do not make it!

There is nothing worse than making a promise to someone and then not keeping it. The promise can be large or small, but it does not matter. Keep your promises!

Liking someone is sometimes harder than loving someone

This may seem counter intuitive, but loving someone should be unconditional while liking someone can absolutely be conditional! Some good friends of ours told us about this concept and how they would affirm their relationship standing by saying "I like you my wife" or "I like you my husband".

Because we are all flawed human beings, we are bound to get on each other's nerves every now and them. Sometimes it is an annoying habit, other times it is a pithy remark or snide comment we make. Perhaps it can even be a "cross" look"

Whatever the case may be, strive towards liking others as well as loving them.

Be what you want others to become

This one seems simple, but is very difficult to execute in real life. It is easy to hold people to expectations that we ourselves are not willing to demonstrate or live by.

Kill them with kindness

While some people in life will view kindness as weakness, you can ultimately persuade and win over most people with kindness. It is easy to lash out and be rude. Kindness requires patience, forethought, and discipline.

People always remember how you make them feel

This is a quote from Maya Angelou I heard many years ago and found to be very true. People may not always remember what you did or said, but they will always remember how you made them feel. Strive to encourage and lift people up wherever you go and wherever you are.

Do not wish the time away - it will pass quickly enough

It is so easy to transition through the different phases of life and hope that the time will pass quickly so you can move on to something new and different. This is especially true with your children.

You will have them in diapers and crawling and wish they could walk. They will be walking and you wish they could talk. They will begin talking and you wish they could dress themselves. They will dress themselves and you wish they could fix their own breakfast.

This goes on and on, and instead of cherishing the season you are in, you wish the time away. Then the day comes when they have moved on completely and you will wish they were younger again.

Cherish every movement, trial and challenge. In many instances it may be the only time you have to address it.

One day I came home late from a very long and hard day at work. I was exhausted!! My youngest son can running out the door to greet me that evening. In his hand he had two empty jars. He wanted me to go catching fire-flies with him right then. I honestly only wanted to eat dinner and go to bed at that moment. However, I remembered my own advice and we went catching fire-flies. It was fun and memorable activity that did not really take that much time. I can vividly remember thinking that this may be the only time in his life that he asks me to catch fire-flies and I did not want to miss that opportunity. Do not let time pass you by.

If possible, live at peace with everyone

This is from Romans 12:18. Pick and choose your battles carefully. There are few thing in life that are worth "falling on your sword" over. There are certainly times to fight and defend, but don't go looking for fights.

I have a good friend of mine who lives a miserable existence because he is always doing battle with someone.   It is just painful to watch and listen to at times.

Practice what you preach

This is especially true in front of your children.   They watch everything you say and do and will know you are a hypocrite in a minute.

Pay it forward

We all need help from time to time.   While you may not be able to payback the person who helped you, you can certainly help others as you grow and mature.

Everyone is either in a storm, coming out of a storm or heading into a storm

Knowing this will help you to better deal with people and how they are acting and reacting. Many times when someone is lashing out it is because there are other things going on in their life that you are not aware of. This does not make their behavior acceptable, but can certainly help explain why they are acting that way.

Just because everybody else is doing it, does not make it right

To follow this advice you have to have a very clear vision of your priorities and how you choose to live your life.   Without this, then you will be "blowing in the wind" and following the crowd.

We have found that in very few instances do we want to follow the crowd.

Do not accept unsolicited advice, but seek wise counsel from those you trust

In your lifetime you will get much unsolicited advice (and most of it will be useless). I always thought it was very funny to get advice on raising our four children from people who had no children. We sought out older and wiser couples who had lots of successful children and families and get their advice and opinions.

Seek out wise counsel from those who have walked the path you are on.

Do not eat spaghetti or ribs on the first date

Now I know this seems silly, but it is really great advice. Spaghetti is just messy and you are most likely to make a mess and get it all over yourself and not make a very good impression.

Everybody has a crazy Uncle/Aunt - don't hold it against that person

We do not get to choose who our parents or relatives are in life. Do not hold it against someone if they have some kind of crazy family member. You should love them for them.

Find a mentor for all aspects of your life - work, relationships, spiritual, physical and mental

A mentor is someone who you can ask those tough questions and they will help you because they want you to do well and succeed. If you are lucky you can find a mentor who can help you with several different aspects listed above.

One of my mentors was an incredible Christian business man who was able to offer advice on spiritual, work, and relationships.

Remember that a mentor should be someone that you trust completely!

Also, it is important for everyone to have a "mentee" as well. You should be giving back and pouring into someone else's life.

Beware of the five time killers

1. Job
2. Cell Phone
3. TV
4. Surfing the Web
5. Hobbies

None of these five things are bad, however if you spend too much time on any of these, your relationships will suffer. You only have 24 hours in each day; it is up to you to use them wisely.

Have someone in your life who is your encourager/cheerleader

We all need encouragement as we walk through this life. Find someone whom you trust and can offer you ongoing encouragement.

Think less of yourself and focus on others

There is a word for this, it is called humility. This is easier said than done, but focusing on the needs, wants and desires of others and serving them is a way to show you truly love and care for them.

Marriage

Do not break faith with your spouse

This means do not fool around with someone else! It is never safe to flirt with someone else. It will only lead to disaster and ruin.

Beware of Social Networking with the opposite Sex

Too many people fall into the trap of connecting with an "old flame" from high school or college and one thing leads to another and before you know it, you are unfaithful to your spouse. Avoid this trap by not becoming "friends" with members of the opposite sex. Extreme advice, but necessary!

Continue to date you spouse every week

This is great advice I got early in my marriage. Do not make the mistake and think that a date has to be something complicated and fancy. It can be as simple a meal at Chick-fil-a without the kids. The goal is to spend some "alone time" with your spouse and re-connect with them.

If possible you should also strive to get away for a long weekend a couple of times a year (this is even truer when kids come along). These are weekends to unwind and reconnect with your true love. This is one tool for keeping your relationship fresh and growing.

You cannot change your spouse - you can only change yourself.

Do not waste time trying to change your spouse. It is a futile effort. Spend your time changing yourself. If you want your spouse to be more romantic, then you be more romantic. If you want your spouse to be a better listener, then become a better listener yourself.

Change yourself and pray to God that He will change your spouse, or change your attitude toward your spouse.

Do not cry on the shoulder of someone of the opposite sex who is not your spouse.

This is asking for trouble.   Be there for your buddy, but not his wife!

Do not marry someone who is not a Christian

The bible is very clear that as Christians we should not be "unequally yoked" with non-believers.   Marriage is difficult enough without the two of you not having the same faith and spiritual walk.
2 Corinthians 6:14

Spend at least a year together (going through all the seasons and major holidays together) before getting engaged

You will want to observe your potential future spouse (and their family) for this length of time, because you might be fooled for a short season but over the course of a year you will get to fully know all the aspects of this person.   Better safe than sorry.

Get to know you future in-laws before you get engaged, you do not just marry the person, and you marry the family.

I have seen many friends end up in very bad situations with families that are in turmoil. Be very careful and thoughtful before you leap into engagement and marriage.

Don't go to bed angry

This from Ephesians 4:26.   You should work out your problems and issues and not sleep them away.   First of all, you probably won't be able to sleep, and secondly, the problem will just fester and get worse instead of better.   Confront the issue and work out the problems.

You have to work at your marriage relationship every day!

Relationships are a job and you need to show up everyday ready for work.   You have to maintain a relationship just like you maintain a car.   Change the oil, rotate the tires, check the brakes, get a tune up, etc. etc.

Listen without solving

This is for all the husbands and fathers who think our wives and daughters want solutions.   What they really want is for us to listen without solving.   I actually ask my Bride if she wants me to listen or solve.   Invariably, she just wants me to listen.   It does take a burden off of me and makes it easier to just listen.   This is a learned skill set for me.   It does not come naturally.

Kiss your spouse a minimum of three times each day -

This is a good way to stay connected in this crazy busy life.   Kiss them goodbye in the morning, kiss them hello when you see them again and finally kiss them again good night.   Remember, this is just a minimum suggestion.   :)

Do not get married if you or your future spouse is heavily in debt

The first years of marriage are hard enough without the burden of debt.   Money and finances are one of the key things that couple will argue and fight about.   If you can eliminate debt early on, then this removes a potential stumbling block in your marriage.   Get rid of the debt and then get married.

Learn to use the following words in your marriage

"I'm sorry"
"I was wrong"
"I forgive you"
"Thank you"

Lean on the strengths of your spouse

You cannot do it all! I know that is a shock to many of you, but nobody is that good.   You spouse has skills and abilities that you do not.   Learn to trust your spouse and lean into their strengths.   The two of you together are a more powerful and effective team.

Do not threaten divorce or leaving

Be committed to your marriage and your spouse.   There will be ups and downs in every marriage, but your mindset should be commitment.

Dance with her every chance you get

Take the opportunity to dance with her. She will love it!

Hold her hand

Take every opportunity to hold her hand. It is a small thing that shows you love her and makes her feel loved.

Walk with her

Don't walk ahead of her, walk by her side. Holding her hand is a good way to make sure you walk together

Go to weddings with her

She will love going to wedding, and I know most guys do not enjoy this activity. However, it is a great opportunity to spend time with her in a romantic setting. You can also dance with her!

Open doors for her

This is just a basic thing you should do every day, and teach your sons to do as well.

Flowers on Tuesday is always a good thing

The whole idea of buying her flowers on Tuesday is that you are getting her flowers, just because you love her. If she does not like flowers, then get chocolate or something that she likes. Surprise her and tell her how much you love her.

Do not forget birthdays or anniversaries

Do whatever you have to do to remember these dates.   Make that day special. For the "big" anniversaries, try to plan a getaway and spend time together.   "Big" anniversaries are 1,5,10, 20, 25 etc.

Tell her each day how beautiful and special she is to you

Constantly remind your bride that she is beautiful in your eyes and the love of your life.

Use every form of communication to tell her you love her - face to face, phone, text, social media, written note etc.

Get creative in how you tell your bride how much you love her. Don't just say it, but send her that sweet text message, or actually write her a note and put it in her purse for her to "discover".

Help her with the difficult tasks that she does not enjoy

Find out the task that she does not like or enjoy and help out. My bride does not like grocery shopping so I take care of that for our family. It is a small thing, but goes a long way to helping her out.

If you want her to enjoy sports, tell her the personal stories of the players.

She will want to make an emotional connection with the team to be engaged. Share some of the personal story lines on the team or coaching staff and that will help.

Be the spiritual leader of your house.

Lead your family in worship, prayer and service.

Protect her from harmful family relationships

You bride may have difficult or even harmful family relationships. Remember that you always take her side and your goal is to protect her. We have seen relationships where the mother or father tries to exert undue influence or pressure and this is where you can help.

Encourage your spouse when they are hurting, sick, tired or depressed.

Sometimes this will be with soothing words, other times it will be acts of love and kindness, and still other times it will just mean you are by their side.

Complete the "Honey Do" list

It is not just enough to complete the "honey do" list; make sure you clean up the mess as well.

If you are running late, let your spouse know.

This is just common curtesy.   You do not want them to worry needlessly and it is rude if you do not let them know you are running late.

Tell her about the details and events of your day

While you may not feel like talking about your day or giving a down load on everything you did, she is very interested in the details. Make the effort to remember key thoughts and details and share with her.

Learn to fight fair

- No yelling and screaming
- Stick to the issue at hand
- Do not bring up past transgressions
- No name calling or sarcasm
- Work hard at listening
- Don't fight in front of the kids!
- Choose the right time (very early or very late is bad)
- Don't go to bed without resolution
- Take responsibility
- No silent treatment - there must be dialog

Share your hopes dreams and desires

You are partners for life. Share all of your hopes, dreams and desires. Bring your spouse fully into your world.

Make dating and time together a priority

Just because you are married does not mean you stop dating your bride. Continue to date her on a weekly basis.   Strive to get away for a couple of long weekends every year.   You need to make time investments in your relationship to help it grow and improve.

Set financial goals and priorities together

These goals are very important especially for the financial area of your life. You will need to be aligned on your priorities and spending. Money and finances can be a key area of contention in any relationship, so work hard to remove any barriers and obstacles.

Rules for a happy marriage: Unknown

1. Never both be angry at the same time.
2. Never yell at each other unless the house is on fire.
3. If one of you has to win an argument, let it be your spouse.
4. If you have to criticize, do it lovingly.
5. Never bring up mistakes from the past.
6. Neglect the whole world rather than each other.
7. Never go to sleep with an argument unsettled.
8. At least once a day say a kind word or pay a compliment to your spouse.
9. When you have done something wrong, admit it and ask for forgiveness.
10. It takes two to make a quarrel, and the one in the wrong is usually the one who does the most talking."
-Unknown

Children

Hug your children early and often

Hugs are how you say "I love you" without saying anything at all.

Your children will disappoint you, love them anyway

Love them unconditionally, but that does not mean you have to agree with their choices and decisions. Be prepared to have the tough conversations and stick to your choices and values.

Do not try to live vicariously through your children

Let you kids follow their own path and bent.   They may not want to be the ballerina you were or the football player you could have been. Expose them to many different activities and see where they shine. You just might be surprised.

Never fall in love with you son's girlfriend or daughter's boyfriend

You do not want to fall in love with them until after they are actually married.   Up until that point, everything is temporary!   You are setting yourself up for headache and heartache if you do.

Always be in alignment on rewards and discipline for kids

Kids are incredible and are some of the best tacticians in the world. They know how to divide and conquer when it comes to dealing with their parents.   If you stand together and are aligned on rewards and discipline then the kids will be in line.

Do not disagree in front of the children

Kids are wonderful at pitting one parent against the other. Have a united front and do not disagree in front of the children. Support each other and decide ahead of time to not let the children divide you.

Try to always keep the lines of communication open with your children (especially when they stray)

When our oldest son decided go down a life path that we did not agree with, we followed advice that we had received from other families who had been down this road before us.   We kept the lines of communication open and showed unconditional love.   This did not mean that we agreed with his choices, but we wanted him to know that we would always be there for him and we were always available to talk.   We walked this path for a year.   We are very glad we talked, texted and e-mailed with our son during this period.

After a year, he made a turn around and better choices.   It was a tough year, but we would not do it differently.

Always help with the kids at bedtime

Do not be absent during bed time. Help get the kids ready, this takes a lot of work when they are small.

Eat meals together as a family as much as possible

I know in this crazy world we live in today that this is tough to do, but make the effort to connect as a family around the table.

Let your children solve problems by themselves

While we can be close by to offer assistance (if they ask or we see they have become completely stuck), it is important for their learning and confidence to learn how to solve problems.   One day you will not be by their side and they will need the skills, wisdom and knowledge to solve problems for themselves.

Set the example for who you want your kids to marry

Be the man you want your daughters to marry. Be the woman you want your sons to marry. Model this behavior and know they are watching all the time.

Do not let the children come between you (literally)

The children can sit on either side of you, but not between you. This may seem like a small and trivial thing, but it goes a long way towards letting the kids know that your spouse comes first in the marriage and has primary importance. One day (hopefully), the children will all be grown and gone and it will just be the two of you again. Therefore, don't let the children come between you now or in the future

Risk taking should be encouraged

I remember reading an article about people in their 90's and they were asked what they would change and or do differently. At the top of their list was taking more risk! They regretted not trying different things and challenging themselves.

Your children should be encouraged to try to stretch themselves in all areas of their life: Physical, Mental, Spiritual, Monetary and Relational

One of the best ways to teach them about risk is to model this behavior for them to see. Teach them how to take risk in a wise and measured way.

Failure is OK - Learn to embrace it!

Along with risk taking is the fact that failure is going to happen. You should teach them to embrace the failure as a learning opportunity and be sure to use this time to love and encourage them.

Always chaperone and choose to be the responsible adult in the room

Whether it is a party, dance or other social activity, decide now that you are going to chaperone and be the responsible adult. Do not trust that the other parents will be responsible.

Trust you parental instinct

If it does not feel right, then it probably isn't. When you parental radar goes off, listen to your instincts and trust them.

Set clear boundaries and enforce them consistently

Your children have to know what the boundaries are in life and the consequences of crossing those boundaries. Remember that parenting is not a democracy. The children do not get a vote! Here are some areas where you will want to set boundaries (this list is not exhaustive)

- Food and meal time
- Chores and expectations of every family member
- Study habits
- Bed time
- Dating
- Alcohol and drinking
- Social Media
- Web surfing
- Cell Phone usage
- Respecting authority

Remember that setting boundaries is all about teaching your children, safety, responsibility, choices and consequences. It is much easier to not set boundaries and let your children do whatever they want. When they are young we have a word for that - BRAT!

Obviously many of these boundaries will change as your child grows and matures. They key to remember is that you are the adult and they are the child.

Think about it this way; as you drive down the road there are clear boundaries and rules that the authorities (local, state, or federal), have put up to keep everyone safe: guard rails, speed limits, directional signs, traffic signals, barriers to separate flow of traffic, etc. etc.

That is a lot barriers and rules for driving! How much more important is your child!!

Be an enthusiastic encourager

Come along side your child and encourage them no matter what they are doing. They will have plenty of nay sayers in their life. Don't be one of them. You should be their biggest cheerleader and supporter

Teach your children to take responsibility

This piece of advice is very deep! You have to start this at a young age and you never stop teaching them this lesson until they are grown and gone from home (and even sometimes beyond that).

They should learn to take responsibility for their:

- **Actions**
- **Words**
- **Deeds**
- **Work**
- **Family**
- **Body**
- **Thoughts**

They need to clearly understand the rewards and consequences of not taking responsibility.

Do not become your child's best friend

Your child does not need another best friend. They need an adult who will love them and care enough about them to appropriately discipline them when necessary.   They need someone who will tell them NO when everyone else is saying YES. They need a parent who is not willing to let them choose a poor path or make fatal decisions. It might be more fun to be their friend, but proper parenting is not about having fun all the time. It is about building responsible adults for the future.

Come alongside them in the areas where they want to excel

If you child loves singing - then let them sing, if sports, then pursue that. It can be crafts, chess, robotics, writing, dancing, etc. etc. They may want to walk a path that is different from yours. That is ok. I have four children and all four of them have very different desires. It is very important that I do not try to make them "mini-me". They need to grow and develop into their own person.

Everyone will offer you advice on how to raise your children

Be polite, nod and forget most of the unsolicited advice you will receive. There is a lot of bad advice out there from people who don't have a clue about raising children (which is most people). However, most people think they are doing a great job and they aren't.

Friends

If you leave this life with 3-4 real close friendships, you have done well

Most people know a lot of people and have many acquaintances, but they have few real friends. A real friend is that person who you call at 3am when there is a need and they help without hesitation or question. A real friend is someone who will see you through the entire crisis even when others have grown weary and leave your side. A real friend will help you stay on the straight and narrow path even when their advice and counsel is tough to take.

Ultimately, there will only be a handful of people who fit the bill to be a real friend. Make every attempt to grow and nurture these relationships.

Your job will not take care of you when you are sick. Your friends and family will

What this means is that you should not live to work, but work to live. Choose to invest your time, talents and treasures in your family and friends. When you leave your job, you will soon be forgotten and business will go on without you.

It is the relationships you have with your family and friends that will sustain you in the most difficult days of your life.

You are known by the friends you keep

Be careful about who you choose to let into your world and whose world you chose to enter. "If you lie down with dogs, you will get fleas". Bad people will bring you down quicker than you think.

You have to work at friendships

You have to work to make friendship a reality. It will take time, energy and effort on your part. The more you invest in the friendship, the more you will get out of it.

How to tell if someone is a good friend

A true friend would model these characteristics:

- Loyal
- Trustworthy
- There for you when you are hurting
- There for you when everyone else abandons you
- Want to celebrate your wins in life
- Good listener
- Love you for who you are
- Willing to give you honest feedback (in a loving way)
- Not willing to let you hurt yourself or others
- They always have your best interest in mind
- Go the extra mile for you
- Laugh with you and cry with you

Learn from three great friendships that are modeled in the bible

Jonathan & David - their story is told in 1 Samuel 18-20 and it is a great story of sacrifice, loyalty, trust and protection. Key Verse:

1 Samuel 20:
Then Jonathan said to David, "Whatever you say, I will do for you."

Of course you have to read the entire Book of 1 Samuel to understand the context, but this is an incredible statement by Jonathan

Ruth & Naomi - their story is told in the book of Ruth and it is sweet story of love, loyalty, trust and encouragement. Key verse:

Ruth 1:16-18
But Ruth said, "Do not urge me to leave you or turn back from following you; for where you go, I will go, and where you lodge, I will lodge. Your people shall be my people, and your God, my God. Where you die, I will die, and there I will be buried. Thus may the Lord do to me, and worse, if anything but death parts you and me."

Paul & Barnabas - their story is told throughout the book of Acts. Barnabas was an encourager by nature and he was the first one to really trust Paul and introduce him to the Apostles in Jerusalem. This was a huge leap of faith given Paul's background and history. Key Verse:

Acts 9:27
But Barnabas took hold of him (Paul) and brought him to the apostles and described to them how he had seen the Lord on the road, and that He had talked to him, and how at Damascus he had spoken out boldly in the name of Jesus.

These three friendships are all great models to follow and learn from as you strive to be the very best friend you can be. I found that the key attribute in each story is Loyalty and Trust. These are easy words to say, but much more difficult to achieve.

Quotes on Relationships

"When there is love in a marriage, there is harmony in the home; when there is harmony in the home, there is contentment in the community; when there is contentment in the community, there is prosperity in the nation; when there is prosperity in the nation, there is peace in the world." **Chinese Proverb**

"There is no greater happiness for a man than approaching a door at the end of a day knowing someone on the other side of that door is waiting for the sound of his footsteps." **Ronald Reagan**

"The happy State of Matrimony is, undoubtedly, the surest and most lasting Foundation of Comfort and Love . . . the Cause of all good Order in the World, and what alone preserves it from the utmost Confusion." **Benjamin Franklin**

"Don't marry the person you think you can live with; marry only the individual you think you can't live without." **James C. Dobson**

"Love is a flower which turns into fruit at marriage."
Finnish Proverb

"A good marriage is one which allows for change and growth in the individuals and in the way they express their love." **Pearl Buck**

"Many marriages would be better if the husband and wife clearly understood that they are on the same side." **Zig Ziglar**

"What greater thing is there for two human souls than to feel that they are joined for life to strengthen each other in all labor, to rest on each other in all sorrow, to minister to each other in all pain, to be one with each other in silent, unspeakable memories at the moment of the last parting." **George Eliot**

"Married couples who love each other tell each other a thousand things without talking." **Chinese Proverb**

"The most desired gift of love is not diamonds or roses or chocolate. It's focused attention." **Rick Warren**

"Marriage succeeds only as lifetime commitment with no escape clauses." **Dr. James Dobson**

"There is nothing more admirable than two people who see eye-to-eye keeping house as man and wife, confounding their enemies, and delighting their friends." **Homer**

"It is love that makes the impossible possible." **Indian Proverb**

"Love sees roses without thorns." **German Proverb**

"You know you're in love when you can't fall asleep because reality is finally better than your dreams." **Dr. Seuss**

"No road is long with good company." **Turkish Proverb**

"The First Bond of Society is Marriage." **Cicero**

"We cannot start over but we can begin now and make a new ending." **Zig Ziglar**

"There cannot be greater rudeness than to interrupt another in the current of his discourse." **John Locke**

"To love our neighbor as ourselves is such a truth for regulating human society, that by that alone one might determine all the cases in social morality." **John Locke**

"We have two ears and one mouth, so we should listen more than we say." **Zino of Citium**

"Without friends no one would choose to live, though he had all other goods." **Aristotle**

"Be kind, for everyone you meet is fighting a hard battle." **Plato**

"Write your injuries in dust, your benefits in marble." **Ben Franklin**

"He who is not a good servant will not be a good master." **Plato**

"Be civil to all; sociable to many; familiar with few; friend to one; enemy to none." **Ben Franklin**

"Never discourage anyone... who continually makes progress, no matter how slow." **Plato**

"You can discover more about a person in an hour of play than in a year of conversation." **Plato**

"Be slow to fall into friendship; but when thou art in, continue firm and constant." **Socrates**

"When you see a worthy person, endeavor to emulate him. When you see an unworthy person, then examine your inner self." **Confucius**

"Have no friends not equal to yourself." **Confucius**

"Don't complain about the snow on your neighbor's roof when your own doorstep is unclean" **Confucius**

"We must all hang together, or assuredly, we shall all hang separately." **Ben Franklin**

"Consideration for others is the basic of a good life, a good society." **Confucius**

"Anyone can become angry. That is easy. But to be angry with the right person, to the right degree, at the right time, for the right purpose and in the right way that is not easy." **Aristotle**

"The best friend is the man who in wishing me well wishes it for my sake". **Aristotle**

"He who cannot be a good follower cannot be a good leader." **Aristotle**

"Remember not only to say the right thing in the right place, but far more difficult still, to leave unsaid the wrong thing at the tempting moment." **Ben Franklin**

"A great relationship doesn't happen because of the love you had in the beginning, but how well you continue building love until the end. " **Unknown**

"A great relationship is about two things, first, find out the similarities, second, respect the differences. " **Unknown**

"Eighty percent of life's satisfaction comes from meaningful relationships. " **Brian Tracy**

"A true relationship is when you can tell each other anything and everything. No secrets and no lies." **Unknown**

"All relationships have one law. Never make the one you love feel alone, especially when you're there." **Unknown**

"Our greatest joy and our greatest pain comes in our relationships with others" **Stephen R. Covey**

"The quality of your life is the quality of your relationships. " **Anthony Robbins**

"The ultimate test of a relationship is to disagree but hold hands" **Unknown**

"A real friend is one who walks in when the rest of the world walks out." **Unknown**

Make a friend when you don't need one. **Jamaican proverb**

"No better relation than a prudent and faithful friend. " **Ben Franklin**

"You never really know your friends from your enemies until the ice breaks." **Eskimo Proverb**

"There is nothing on this earth more to be prized than true friendship." **Thomas Aquinas**

"Walking with a friend in the dark is better than walking alone in the light." **Helen Keller**

"Friendship is born at that moment when one man says to another: What! You too? I thought that no one but myself" **CS Lewis**

Wishing to be friends is quick work, but friendship is a slow ripening fruit. **Aristotle**

"Many marriages would be better if the husband and the wife clearly understood that they are on the same side" **Zig Ziglar**

"Marriage is more than finding the right person. It is being the right person. " **Unknown**

"There is no more lovely, friendly, charming relationship, communion or company than a good marriage." **Martin Luther**

"In marriage do thou be wise: prefer the person before money, virtue before beauty, the mind before the body; then thou hast a wife, a friend, a companion, a second self." **William Penn**

"There is nothing on this earth more to be prized than true friendship." **Thomas Aquinas**

"Friendship is the source of the greatest pleasures, and without friends even the most agreeable pursuits become tedious."
Thomas Aquinas

"The happy man in this life needs friends." **Thomas Aquinas**

"It is not so much our friends' help that helps us as the confident knowledge that they will help us." **Epicurus**

"Of all the things which wisdom acquires to produce the blessedness of the complete life, for the greatest is the possession of friendship."
Epicurus

"We should look for someone to eat and drink with before looking for something to eat and drink." **Epicurus**

"To eat and drink without a friend is to devour like the lion and the wolf."
Epicurus

"To know what people really think, pay attention to what they do, rather than what they say." **René Descartes**

"Wishing to be friends is quick work, but friendship is slow ripening fruit."
Aristotle

"What is a friend A single soul dwelling in two bodies". **Aristotle**

"A friend is a second self." **Aristotle**

"Friendship is essentially a partnership." **Aristotle**

In poverty and other misfortunes of life, true friends are a sure refuge.
Aristotle

"A friend to all is a friend to none." **Aristotle**

"What you do not want others to do to you, do not do to others."
Confucius

"To love someone is to identify with them." **Aristotle**

"Silence is the true friend that never betrays." **Confucius**

"To be wronged is nothing unless you continue to remember it." **Confucius**

"To know what is right and not do it is the worst cowardice." **Confucius**

"Before you embark on a journey of revenge, dig two graves."
Confucius

"TszeKung asked, saying, is there one word which may serve as a rule of practice for all one's life? The Master said, Is not Reciprocity such a word? What you do not want done to yourself, do not do to others".
Confucius

"The best way to cheer yourself is to cheer somebody else up." **Einstein**

"There is no such thing as a lover's oath". **Plato**

"Friends have all things in common." **Plato**

"Be courteous to all, but intimate with few, and let those few be well tried before you give them your confidence." **George Washington**

"I don't need a friend who changes when I change and who nods when I nod; my shadow does that much better." **Plutarch**

"Wishing to be friends is quick work, but friendship is a slow ripening fruit". **Aristotle**

If you go to a donkey's house, don't talk about ears.
Jamaican Proverb

A friend in need is a friend indeed.

A friend who shares is a friend who cares.

A man is known by the company he keeps.

"If you want to go fast, go alone. If you want to go far, go together."
African Proverb

"Man must cease attributing his problems to his environment, and learn again to exercise his will – his personal responsibility."
Albert Einstein

"It is a painful thing to look at your own trouble and know that you yourself and no one else has made it." **Sophocles**

Bible Verses on Relationships

Matthew 22:36-40
"Teacher, which is the great commandment in the Law?" And He said to him, "'You shall love the Lord your God with all your heart, and with all your soul, and with all your mind.' This is the great and foremost commandment. The second is like it, 'You shall love your neighbor as yourself.' On these two commandments depend the whole Law and the Prophets."
Deuteronomy 6:4-5
"Hear, O Israel! The Lord is our God, the Lord is one! You shall love the Lord your God with all your heart and with all your soul and with all your might.

Leviticus 19:18
You shall not take vengeance, nor bear any grudge against the sons of your people, but you shall love your neighbor as yourself; I am the Lord.

Ecclesiastes 4:9-12
Two are better than one because they have a good return for their labor. For if either of them falls, the one will lift up his companion. But woe to the one who falls when there is not another to lift him up. Furthermore, if two lie down together they keep warm, but how can one be warm alone? And if one can overpower him who is alone, two can resist him. A cord of three strands is not quickly torn apart.

Ephesians 4:26
Be angry, and yet do not sin; do not let the sun go down on your anger,

Proverbs 17:17
A friend loves at all times, And a brother is born for adversity.

Proverbs 18:24
A man of too many friends comes to ruin, But there is a friend who sticks closer than a brother.

Proverbs 27:6
Faithful are the wounds of a friend, But deceitful are the kisses of an enemy.

John 15:13
Greater love has no one than this, that one lay down his life for his friends

Proverbs 27:14
He who blesses his friend with a loud voice early in the morning, It will be reckoned a curse to him.

John 15:13
Greater love has no one than this, that one lay down his life for his friends.

Proverbs 27:10
Do not forsake your own friend or your father's friend, And do not go to your brother's house in the day of your calamity; Better is a neighbor who is near than a brother far away.

Malachi 2:15
.... Take heed then to your spirit, and let no one deal treacherously against the wife of your youth.

Ephesians 5:33
Nevertheless, each individual among you also is to love his own wife even as himself, and the wife must see to it that she respects her husband.

Romans 12:9-10
Let love be without hypocrisy. Abhor what is evil; cling to what is good. Be devoted to one another in brotherly love; give preference to one another in honor;

Ephesians 6:4
Fathers, do not provoke your children to anger, but bring them up in the discipline and instruction of the Lord.

Proverbs 15:22
Without consultation, plans are frustrated, But with many counselors they succeed.

Ephesians 6
Children, obey your parents in the Lord, for this is right. Honor your father and mother (which is the first commandment with a promise), so that it may be well with you, and that you may live long on the earth.

1 Corinthians 7:2-4
But because of immoralities, each man is to have his own wife, and each woman is to have her own husband. The husband must fulfill his duty to his wife, and likewise also the wife to her husband. The wife does not have authority over her own body, but the husband does; and likewise also the husband does not have authority over his own body, but the wife does.

Proverbs 5:18
Let your fountain be blessed,
And rejoice in the wife of your youth

2 Corinthians 6:14
Do not be bound together with unbelievers; for what partnership have righteousness and lawlessness, or what fellowship has light with darkness?

1 Peter 4:8
Above all, keep fervent in your love for one another, because love covers a multitude of sins.

Genesis 2:24
For this reason a man shall leave his father and his mother, and be joined to his wife; and they shall become one flesh.

Ephesians 5:22-32
Wives, be subject to your own husbands, as to the Lord. For the husband is the head of the wife, as Christ also is the head of the church, He Himself being the Savior of the body. But as the church is subject to Christ, so also the wives ought to be to their husbands in everything.
Husbands, love your wives, just as Christ also loved the church and gave Himself up for her, so that He might sanctify her, having cleansed her by the washing of water with the word, that He might present to Himself the church in all her glory, having no spot or wrinkle or any such thing; but that she would be holy and blameless. So husbands ought also to love their own wives as their own bodies. He who loves his own wife loves himself; for no one ever hated his own flesh, but nourishes and cherishes it, just as Christ also does the church, because we are members of His body. For this reason a man shall leave his father and mother and shall be joined to his wife, and the two shall become one flesh. This mystery is great; but I am speaking with reference to Christ and the church.

1 Corinthians 13:4-7
Love is patient, love is kind and is not jealous; love does not brag and is not arrogant, does not act unbecomingly; it does not seek its own, is not provoked, does not take into account a wrong suffered, does not rejoice in unrighteousness, but rejoices with the truth; bears all things, believes all things, hopes all things, endures all things.

Hebrews 13:4
Marriage is to be held in honor among all, and the marriage bed is to be undefiled; for fornicators and adulterers God will judge.

1 Peter 3:7
You husbands in the same way, live with your wives in an understanding way, as with someone weaker, since she is a woman; and show her honor as a fellow heir of the grace of life, so that your prayers will not be hindered.

Mark 10:9
What therefore God has joined together let no man separate."

Ecclesiastes 9:9
Enjoy life with the woman whom you love all the days of your fleeting life which He has given to you under the sun[b]; for this is your reward in life and in your toil in which you have labored under the sun.

Ephesians 4:32
Be kind to one another, tender-hearted, forgiving each other, just as God in Christ also has forgiven you

Exodus 20: 3-17

The Ten Commandments

1. *"You shall have no other gods before Me.*

2. *"You shall not make for yourself an idol, or any likeness of what is in heaven above or on the earth beneath or in the water under the earth*

3. *"You shall not take the name of the Lord your God in vain, for the Lord will not leave him unpunished who takes His name in vain.*

4. *"Remember the Sabbath day, to keep it holy.*

5. *"Honor your father and your mother, that your days may be prolonged in the land which the Lord your God gives you.*

6. *"You shall not murder.*

7. *"You shall not commit adultery.*

8. *"You shall not steal.*

9. *"You shall not bear false witness against your neighbor.*

10. *"You shall not covet your neighbor's house;*

Faith, Prayer & Worship

There is nothing more important in life than Faith in Jesus Christ as your Lord and Savior. The advice I offer here is about accepting on faith that Jesus is the Son of God, who died for our sins, rose on the third day, and will return one day for his church.

Prayer is one of the offensive weapons we have in our arsenal to defend our self in this world and to make our petitions known to God. Prayer is also a key tool for encouraging and lifting up the needs of others.

One of my all-time favorite quotes (from one of my favorite authors) C.S. Lewis. He basically said that Jesus was either - Lord, Lunatic or Liar.

"I am trying here to prevent anyone saying the really foolish thing that people often say about Him: I'm ready to accept Jesus as a great moral teacher, but I don't accept his claim to be God. That is the one thing we must not say. A man who was merely a man and said the sort of things Jesus said would not be a great moral teacher. He would either be a lunatic — on the level with the man who says he is a poached egg — or else he would be the Devil of Hell. You must make your choice. Either this man was, and is, the Son of God, or else a madman or something worse. You can shut him up for a fool, you can spit at him and kill him as a demon or you can fall at his feet and call him Lord and God, but let us not come with any patronizing nonsense about his being a great human teacher. He has not left that open to us. He did not intend to." CS Lewis

Wisdom comes from the Bible

Become a student of the bible and seek God's wisdom. Start with the proverbs of Solomon and take those lessons to heart first. As you progress in your study, you will find the Bible is THE guide for your life and has the answers you need for the questions you seek.

Find a good church home where you can plug in and be connected

No matter where you are living, seek out a good church. Being in fellowship with a body of believers will not only help you assimilate into the community, it will also be there to support and comfort you in times of need. Become an active member and attend regular services each week.

Remember the two commandments - Love others as yourself, and love God with all you heart, mind, body and soul

Jesus taught that all 10 of the commandment boiled down to just these two simple principles. If you can keep these at the forefront of your thinking each and every day, it will start to transform how you act and interact with others.

When you don't know what to do, do what your know to do

This means that when you are in doubt, fear or unbelief, remember this saying. What it means is that you should continue to pray and study the bible, continue to trust God and continue to be in fellowship with other believers. Those are all good things to do in every phase of your life.

If God is for you, who can be against you?

This is from Roman 8:31. What a great verse to encourage and strengthen your faith in God. Do not fear or worry about this world. God has your back.

Let the fruits of the spirit guide your life

This is from Galatians 5:22-23. Love, Joy, Peace, Patience, Kindness, Goodness, Faithfulness, Gentleness and Self-Control. These are the key character traits of a Christian.

A person walking with God is always in the majority

I am not sure where I read this, but it has stuck with me ever since I did read it. It is a corollary to Romans 8:31 above.

Read a Chapter of Proverbs each day

There are 31 chapters in the book of Proverbs. There is one chapter for every day of the week. It is a great habit to get into. I have been doing this for a very long time and somehow the verses never get old.

Serve Others

Look for opportunities to serve others in your church and community. Take the opportunity to serve others with your family as well. This is a great chance to bond and create memories together.

Pray Daily - several times a day if possible

Prayer is an excellent way to wake up in the morning and an excellent way to go to sleep each night. There is no such thing as too much prayer. Be a prayer warrior for others and lift up your prayers and petitions for them.

Teach your children to be prayer warriors, by praying with them

For our children my bride prays with them in the morning and then I lead prayer with them in the evening. It is important to make prayer a priority and to model this for you children and family.

Invest in a good study bible and library of reference materials

Become a student of the bible and dive deep into the word of God. Get some good study guides to help you better understand the bible.

Give of your time, talent and treasure for God's kingdom

This means to invest your whole self into serving God's kingdom work here on earth. You have been uniquely blessed and gifted by God with certain talents and abilities, so use those for His glory. It does not matter if you are a mechanic, doctor, accountant or sales person. You have skills that can be used by your local church and community.

Take the opportunity to go on a short term mission trip

There is no better way to see God working around the world than to go on a short term mission trip. It will really open your eyes to see other people worshiping in their own language.

Do not pray a prayer you are not prepared to be the answer to

So often, we pray for God to intervene in a situation for someone else and we ask for an answer and clear direction. However, we need to be prepared to be the answer to that request. I will tell you that it is such a blessing to be an answer to a prayer and to be the instrument through which God choses to act.

Support Missionaries on the Local, National and International level

Sharing the Good News of gospel of Jesus Christ is a primary function of each Christian. For those individuals and families who enter the mission field, it is critically important that we support them both spiritually (with prayer) as well as financially. It takes money and prayer to move the Gospel around the world.

Learn how to share the Good News of the Gospel

The most important decision someone will make in life is whether to trust Jesus as their personal Lord and Savior.

Start by memorizing the Romans Road to lead other to God:

Romans 3:23
for all have sinned and fall short of the glory of God,

Romans 6:23
For the wages of sin is death, but the free gift of God is eternal life in Christ Jesus our Lord.

Romans 5:8
But God demonstrates His own love toward us, in that while we were yet sinners, Christ died for us.

Romans 10:9-10
that if you confess with your mouth Jesus as Lord, and believe in your heart that God raised Him from the dead, you will be saved; for with the heart a person believes, resulting in righteousness, and with the mouth he confesses, resulting in salvation.

Romans 10:13
for "Whoever will call on the name of the Lord will be saved."

You should have a "Paul", "Barnabas", and "Timothy" in your life

"Paul"- would be your mentor
"Barnabas"- would be your encourager
"Timothy" - would be your mentee

All three of these relationships will help you grow spiritually and draw you closer to God.

One of the best ways to combat selfishness is to be generous

Selfishness is one of the biggest opportunities for Christians to deal with. I have found that the best way to deal with this is to be generous in supporting the church, mission work and local charities. Not only giving, but giving generously!

Learn How to Deal with Temptation

It is not **IF** you will face temptation, it is when you face temptation. You have to decide how you will deal with the temptation before you encounter it.   There are several great bible verses that deal with this area: FLEE is a real option!!

Matthew 26:41
Keep watching and praying that you may not enter into temptation; the spirit is willing, but the flesh is weak."

1 Corinthians 10:13
No temptation has overtaken you but such as is common to man; and God is faithful, who will not allow you to be tempted beyond what you are able, but with the temptation will provide the way of escape also, so that you will be able to endure it.

1 Corinthians 6:18
Flee immorality. Every other sin that a man commits is outside the body, but the [a]immoral man sins against his own body.

James 4:7
Submit therefore to God. Resist the devil and he will flee from you.

1 Corinthians 6:18-20
Flee immorality. Every other sin that a man commits is outside the body, but the immoral man sins against his own body. Or do you not know that your body is a temple of the Holy Spirit who is in you, whom you have from God, and that you are not your own? For you have been bought with a price: therefore glorify God in your body.

2 Timothy 2:22
Now flee from youthful lusts and pursue righteousness, faith, love and peace, with those who call on the Lord from a pure heart.

James 5:16
Therefore, confess your sins to one another, and pray for one another so that you may be healed. The effective prayer of a righteous man can accomplish much.

Hebrews 2:18
For since He Himself was tempted in that which He has suffered, He is able to come to the aid of those who are tempted.

Romans 13:13-14
Let us behave properly as in the day, not in carousing and drunkenness, not in sexual promiscuity and sensuality, not in strife and jealousy. But put on the Lord Jesus Christ, and make no provision for the flesh in regard to its lusts.

Ephesians 6:10-18
Finally, be strong in the Lord and in the strength of His might. Put on the full armor of God, so that you will be able to stand firm against the schemes of the devil. For our struggle is not against flesh and blood, but against the rulers, against the powers, against the world forces of this darkness, against the spiritual forces of wickedness in the heavenly places. Therefore, take up the full armor of God, so that you will be able to resist in the evil day, and having done everything, to stand firm. Stand firm therefore, having girded your loins with truth, and having put on the breastplate of righteousness, and having shod your feet with the preparation of the gospel of peace; in addition to all, taking up the shield of faith with which you will be able to extinguish all the flaming arrows of the evil one. And take the helmet of salvation, and the sword of the Spirit, which is the word of God. With all prayer and petition [d]pray at all times in the Spirit, and with this in view, [be on the alert with all perseverance and petition for all the saints,

You should get your identity from who God says you are

If you are not careful, you will let the world, work, friends, family or other define who you are. They will try to influence your identity and define who you are and what you could and should be, now and in the future.

You should strive to get your identity from God and understand how God sees you. Here are a few verses to help:

Genesis 1:27
God created man in His own image, in the image of God He created him; male and female He created them.

2 Corinthians 5:17
Therefore if anyone is in Christ, he is a new creature; the old things passed away; behold, new things have come.

1 Corinthians 12:27
Now you are Christ's body, and individually members of it.

Philippians 3:20
For our citizenship is in heaven, from which also we eagerly wait for a Savior, the Lord Jesus Christ;

John 1:12
But as many as received Him, to them He gave the right to become children of God, even to those who believe in His name,

1 Peter 2:9
But you are a chosen race, a royal priesthood, a holy nation, a people for God's own possession, so that you may proclaim the excellencies of Him who has called you out of darkness into His marvelous light;

John 15:14-15
(Jesus speaking) *You are My friends if you do what I command you. No longer do I call you slaves, for the slave does not know what his master is doing; but I have called you friends, for all things that I have heard from My Father I have made known to you.*

John 15:5
I am the vine, you are the branches; he who abides in Me and I in him, he bears much fruit, for apart from Me you can do nothing.

1 Corinthians 6:20
For you have been bought with a price: therefore glorify God in your body.

Ephesians 1:7
In Him we have redemption through His blood, the forgiveness of our trespasses, according to the riches of His grace

Ephesians 2:10
For we are His workmanship, created in Christ Jesus for good works, which God prepared beforehand so that we would walk in them.

1 Corinthians 6:19
Or do you not know that your body is a temple of the Holy Spirit who is in you, whom you have from God, and that you are not your own?

Romans 8:37
But in all these things we overwhelmingly conquer through Him who loved us.

Be thankful for what you have

I want to end this chapter with this final piece of advice. We can get so consumed with what we "lack" in this life and what others "have", that we forget to be thankful for what we have! Take some time to list all the things you are thankful for today. I think you will be pleasantly surprised by how many things you have to be thankful for. As I finish this chapter, here are just a few things I am thankful for:

- My beautiful bride!
- Health - ability to walk and move around
- Job
- Food, Clothing and Shelter
- Incredible children
- Friends and family
- Living in a wonderful state and country
- Freedom of worship

It is always easy to envy others and wish for "more", but be thankful for what you have right now.

Quotes on Faith, Prayer & Worship

"For those with faith, no evidence is necessary; for those without it, no evidence will suffice." **Thomas Aquinas**

"In prayer it is better to have a heart without words than words without a heart. " **John Bunyan**

"Faith takes God without any ifs." **D.L. Moody**

"Faith has to do with things that are not seen, and hope with things that are not in hand." **Thomas Aquinas**

"The prayer offered to God in the morning during your quiet time is the key that unlocks the door of the day. Any athlete knows that it is the start that ensures a good finish." **Adrian Rogers**

I know of no better thermometer to your spiritual temperature than this, the measure of the intensity of your prayer.
Charles Spurgeon

We can do nothing without prayer. All things can be done by importunate prayer. It surmounts or removes all obstacles, overcomes every resisting force and gains its ends in the face of invincible hindrances. **E.M. Bounds**

Our prayers run along one road and God's answers by another, and by and by they meet. **Adoniram Judson**

"Prayer is not learned in a classroom but in the closet." **E. M. Bounds**

"A true prayer is an inventory of needs, a catalog of necessities, an exposure of secret wounds, a revelation of hidden poverty."
Charles Spurgeon

"If you want that splendid power in prayer, you must remain in loving, living, lasting, conscious, practical, abiding union with the Lord Jesus Christ." **Charles Spurgeon**

"Prayer is simply a two-way conversation between you and God." **Billy Graham**

"Prayer can never be in excess." **Charles Spurgeon**

If you are strangers to prayer you are strangers to power. **Billy Sunday**

"...True prayer is measured by weight, not by length. A single groan before God may have more fullness of prayer in it than a fine oration of great length." **Charles Spurgeon**

" The word of God is the food by which prayer is nourished and made strong." **E. M. Bounds**

"Faith sees the invisible, believes the unbelievable, and receives the impossible." **Corrie Ten Boom**

"The only way to learn strong faith is to endure great trials." **George Muller**

"When I cannot enjoy the faith of assurance, I live by the faith of adherence." **Matthew Henry**

"Do all the good you can. By all the means you can. In all the ways you can. In all the places you can. At all the times you can. To all the people you can. As long as ever you can." **John Wesley**

"If you want that splendid power in prayer, you must remain in loving, living, lasting, conscious, practical, abiding union with the Lord Jesus Christ." **Charles Spurgeon**

The beginning of anxiety is the end of faith, and the beginning of true faith is the end of anxiety. **George Mueller**

"Prayer is not overcoming God's reluctance, but laying hold of His willingness." **Martin Luther**

"Faith obliterates time, annihilates distance, and brings future things at once into its possession." **Charles Spurgeon**

"Fear can keep us up all night long, but faith makes one fine pillow." **Unknown**

"When you get to the end of all the light you know and it's time to step into the darkness of the unknown, faith is knowing that one of two things shall happen: either you will be given something solid to stand on, or you will be taught how to fly." **Edward Teller**

"If you wish to know God, you must know his Word. If you wish to perceive His power, you must see how He works by his Word. If you wish to know His purpose before it comes to pass, you can only discover it by His Word." **Charles Spurgeon**

"Faith goes up the stairs that love has built and looks out the window which hope has opened" **Charles Spurgeon**

"Faith isn't believing without proof – it's trusting without reservation." **William Sloane Coffin**

"I believe though I do not comprehend, and I hold by faith what I cannot grasp with the mind." **Saint Bernard**

"God isn't looking for people of great faith, but for individuals ready to follow Him" **Hudson Taylor**

"Faith is deliberate confidence in the character of God whose ways you may not understand at the time." **Oswald Chambers**

"The most valuable thing the Psalms do for me is to express the same delight in God which made David dance." **C.S. Lewis**

"God is to be praised with the voice, and the heart should go therewith in holy exultation." **Charles Spurgeon**

"Worship is the believer's response of all that they are – mind, emotions, will, body – to what God is and says and does." **Warren Wiersbe**

Bible verses on Faith, Prayer & Worship

2 Corinthians 5:7
For we walk by faith, not by sight

Romans 10:17
So faith comes from hearing, and hearing by the word of Christ.

Ephesians 2:8-9
For by grace you have been saved through faith; and that not of yourselves, it is the gift of God; not as a result of works, so that no one may boast.

John 14:6
Jesus *said to him, "I am the way, and the truth, and the life; no one comes to the Father but through Me.

Romans 3:23
for all have sinned and fall short of the glory of God,

Romans 6:23
For the wages of sin is death, but the free gift of God is eternal life in Christ Jesus our Lord.

Romans 5:8
But God demonstrates His own love toward us, in that while we were yet sinners, Christ died for us.

Romans 10:13
for "Whoever will call on the name of the Lord will be saved."

John 3:16
"For God so loved the world, that He gave His only begotten Son, that whoever believes in Him shall not perish, but have eternal life.

Ephesians 2:8-9
For by grace you have been saved through faith; and that not of yourselves, it is the gift of God; not as a result of works, so that no one may boast.

Psalms 64:1
Hear my voice, O God, in my prayer: preserve my life from fear of the enemy.

Psalms 84:8
O Lord God of hosts, hear my prayer: give ear, O God of Jacob. Selah.

Matthew 6:9-13
"Pray, then, in this way:
'Our Father who is in heaven,
Hallowed be Your name.
'Your kingdom come.
Your will be done,
On earth as it is in heaven.
'Give us this day our daily bread.
'And forgive us our debts, as we also have forgiven our debtors.
'And do not lead us into temptation, but deliver us from evil.
For Yours is the kingdom and the power and the glory forever. Amen.'

James 5:16
Therefore, confess your sins to one another, and pray for one another so that you may be healed. The effective prayer of a righteous man can accomplish much.

1 Thessalonians 5:16-18
Rejoice always; pray without ceasing; in everything give thanks; for this is God's will for you in Christ Jesus.

Colossians 4:2
Devote yourselves to prayer, keeping alert in it with an attitude of thanksgiving;

Philippians 4:6-7
Be anxious for nothing, but in everything by prayer and supplication with thanksgiving let your requests be made known to God. And the peace of God, which surpasses all comprehension, will guard your hearts and your minds in Christ Jesus.

Psalm 95:6
Come, let us worship and bow down,
Let us kneel before the Lord our Maker.

Isaiah 12:5
Praise the Lord in song, for He has done excellent things;
Let this be known throughout the earth.

Matthew 18:20
For where two or three have gathered together in My name, I am there in their midst."

Hebrews 10:25
not forsaking our own assembling together, as is the habit of some, but encouraging one another; and all the more as you see the day drawing near.

Psalm 132:7
Let us go into His [a]dwelling place;
Let us worship at His footstool.

Job 1:20-21
Then Job arose and tore his robe and shaved his head, and he fell to the ground and worshiped. He said,

"Naked I came from my mother's womb,
And naked I shall return there.
The Lord gave and the Lord has taken away.
Blessed be the name of the Lord."

Psalm 99:5
Exalt the Lord our God
And worship at His footstool;
Holy is He.

Psalm 84:10
For a day in Your courts is better than a thousand outside.
I would rather stand at the threshold of the house of my God
Than dwell in the tents of wickedness.

Psalm 66:44
"All the earth will worship You,
And will sing praises to You;
They will sing praises to Your name." Selah

Education & Learning

We spend 12 years going to elementary, middle and high school and then if we go to college that is an additional 4 years (or longer for some of us). If you get a professional degree then that is 2-3 additional years of school. This does not even take into account becoming a doctor which adds 4 years of medical school and then many more years of learning beyond that.

In other words, we invest a lot of time, money and effort gaining an education to earn a living. You should make every effort to be a student your entire life. Learning never stops and you should never stop learning.

Get as much education as possible; it can never be taken from you

There are a lot of things that can be taken from you, like wealth and possessions, but once you have education and knowledge, that can never be taken from you! It is locked in your head and you have full use of it forever.

Never stop learning

Once you have all the knowledge locked away above, keep adding to it! Your brain has almost infinite capability to add new knowledge and wisdom. Most people stop intentionally learning after high school and college, but I implore you to never stop!

Never stop reading - read 2-4 new books each year

Almost a half of all college graduates never read a book again after college.   Take the time to continue to read and learn.

Learn from others mistakes and experience

It is much better to learn from others and their mistakes than to make them yourself.

In other words, don't make the same mistake twice.   The experiences you gain in life should be building blocks of knowledge that will make you wiser and more knowledgeable.

Seek out wise people and learn from them

Remember that wisdom is not the same as knowledge.   There are plenty of people who are knowledgeable but not wise.   My grandfather was not a knowledgeable or educated man, but he was very wise.

Learn another language

This is a no brainer. The world is shrinking and while English is one of the most spoken languages, you can only help your career by learning a new language.   Here are my suggestions:

- Chinese
- Spanish
- French
- Portuguese
- Hindi
- Arabic
- Russian
- Japanese
- Bengali
- Javanese

Keep a journal

I have found it very helpful to have a journal. You can capture your thoughts and questions as well as review what has happened to in the past.

Make your goal to attain Deans List and Presidents List in college

I wish my parents had told me about this when I started college. Not only does this look good on your resume, it also can help you get a job. Dean's list is generally a 3.5 GPA (grade point average) for the semester. President's list is 4.0 GPA for a semester. That means straight A's.

You will only get as much out as you put in

You have to apply yourself to your education and strive to take it all in. There is a direct correlation between how hard you work and the grades you make and knowledge you gain.

Choose wisdom over experience

This means learning from others and what they have been through. While experience is a good teacher, it is also a costly and sometimes a cruel teacher. I don't have to experience drug usage to know it is bad!

More is caught than taught

This is about raising your children. They are watching you 24/7/365. They know a hypocrite when they see one. Know that they may listen to your words but the will follow your actions. It is important to be very intentional with your children.

Only take 12 hours your first semester in College

Your first semester of college is hard enough without the burden of a full load of classes. Taking 12 hours means you would still be considered "full time" and therefor eligible for Dean's List and Presidents List. It will also mean you are a full-time student for a plethora of other reasons - scholarships, legal, insurance, work-study, etc.

Do yourself a favor and take fewer hours and make great grades your first semester in school. You can also consider extending this to the second semester as well. Then if you take two summer classes (generally easier), you will still be at the same point as your peers (only with better grades hopefully).

Go to a local/junior college the first two years

This is a great way to knock out two years of basic/core requirements stuff (English, history, science etc.).   You can save a ton of money as well as set a great GPA.   Then you transfer to your final college/university.   Nobody will care where you did your first two years; they will only look at the final degree.

In addition, you also may find it easier to get into that university as a transfer student (especially if you made good grades).

Have a large library

These days it can be either a digital library or a real library. Whichever it is, you should know that having a large library is key to keeping your mind sharp and nimble.   I personally like the feel of a real book in my hand.   However, I read some books digitally (usually when I am traveling).   Having a large library also gives your family something to look at and read as well.

Consider your "final" resume even as you start college

What I mean is that you should be thoughtful of the activities you participate in while in college.   Think of the clubs, societies, fraternities/sororities etc.   Don't just be a member/participant, but strive to be a leader.   This will allow you to have something to put on your resume beside your classes.

Other things that will impact your resume and should be top of mind

- GPA - higher is better than lower - keep it above 3.0 at a minimum. Many companies use this as a gauge for allowing an interview.   Most scholarships also require a high GPA.
- Work -you need to work part-time at a minimum during the year and full-time in the summer.   Look for jobs that will give you responsibility - looks good on a resume
- Volunteer activities - try to do something that appeals to you and allows you to give back to your community.
- Internships - start looking for internships at the end of your sophomore year.
- Travel - look for opportunities to travel internationally and or study abroad.

Get your advanced degree while you are young and single

If possible, try to get your Masters/Doctorate while you are still young and single. I can tell you from personal experience it is incredibly difficult to do after you have started a family. I have four children and went back for my MBA in my late 40's and did it, but I wish I had done it while I was in my 20's and single.

Take advantage of your company's education reimbursement

If you are lucky enough to work for a company that offers to reimburse education expenses, then take advantage of it! My company basically paid for almost 50% of my MBA. It takes some effort to wade through the paperwork, but it is well worth the effort.

Apply for lots of scholarships

There are literally thousands of scholarships! Most likely you are eligible for many of them. Take advantage of the "free" money. You have not because you ask not.

Pay Attention in Class and don't be shy

Yes this is obvious advice, but you should do the following in class:

- Take good notes
- Ask questions and participate
- Get to know your professors - many companies use them to find good students
- Do every extra credit assignment
- Challenge the grading especially if you do not think a question is fair or reasonable

Find out about your class or professor before enrolling

Take the opportunity to ask friends and fellow students about a class or professor. Take advantage of your social media and websites that provide ratings. If everybody is telling you to "run away as fast as you can" - this is a pretty good indicator to skip this class or professor.

The smartest student does not always get the best grade

It takes more than "smarts" to make a good grade. You have to be prepared and study. Hard work does pay off when it comes to school.

College is supposed to be hard!!

According to the census bureau, about 30% of the population has a bachelor's degree or higher. A little over half of the students who start college are able to finish in 6 years or less. That means a lot of people are starting college and dropping out and not finishing. I think that many students are not prepared for how hard college is going to be and how much work, study and preparation are necessary to succeed. College is a marathon and not a sprint. Prepare your heart and mind now for the hard work and you will not be surprised when it is difficult.

Treat you college education like a job

Go to your "job" every day from 8-5. Set that time aside for classes, study, research and catching up or more importantly - getting ahead. If you do this Monday - Friday, then you should not have to work that hard at nights and weekends.

Avoid the obvious dangers of college

Here are some obvious things to avoid:

- Skipping class
- Falling behind course work
- Not taking advantage of all the resources available
- Not talking to counselors
- Not getting enough sleep
- Not eating well
- Parties!
- Trying to do too much
- Not studying hard enough and taking each class seriously
- Taking out student loans
- Not working
- Getting into a serious relationship

To avoid these dangers you need to have a plan and discipline.

A college degree generally leads to a higher standard of living

In 2013, about 72.1 percent of 25- to 34-year-olds with a bachelor's or higher degree in the labor force had year-round, full-time jobs, compared with 67.5 percent of those with an associate's degree, 59.0 percent of those with some college education, 61.7 percent of high school completers, and 53.3 percent of those without a high school diploma or its equivalent . In 2014, a smaller percentage of 20- to 24-year-olds with a bachelor's degree or higher were unemployed than were their peers with lower levels of education (source).

In 2013, median earnings for full-time year-round working young adults ages 25–34 with a bachelor's degree were $48,500, while the median was $23,900 for those without a high school diploma or its equivalent, $30,000 for those with a high school diploma or its equivalent, and $37,500 for those with an associate's degree. In other words, young adults with a bachelor's degree earned more than twice as much as those without a high school diploma or its equivalent (103 percent more) and 62 percent more than young adult high school completers. Additionally, in 2013 median earnings for young adults with a master's or higher degree were $59,600, some 23 percent more than the median for young adults with a bachelor's degree.

Source: http://nces.ed.gov/fastfacts

Quotes on Education & Learning

"Formal education will make you a living; self-education will make you a fortune." **Jim Rohn**

"An investment in knowledge pays the best interest."
Ben Franklin

"Empty pockets never held anyone back. Only empty heads and empty hearts can do that." **Norman Vincent Peale**

"If a man empties his purse into his head, no one can take it from him. An investment in knowledge always pays the best interest."
Ben Franklin

"Genius without education is like silver in the mine." **Ben Franklin**

"Reading furnishes the mind only with material for knowledge; it is thinking that makes what we read ours." **John Locke**

"Being ignorant is not so much a shame as being unwilling to learn."
Ben Franklin

"Learn from yesterday, live for today, hope for tomorrow. The important thing is to not stop questioning." **Einstein**

"The direction in which education starts a man will determine his future life." **Plato**

"Bodily exercise, when compulsory, does no harm to the body; but knowledge which is acquired under compulsion obtains no hold on the mind." **Plato**

"Ignorance, the root and the stem of every evil." **Plato**

"Employ your time in improving yourself by other men's writings, so that you shall gain easily what others have labored hard for." **Socrates**

"As for me, all I know is that I know nothing." **Socrates**

"If you can't explain it to a six year old, you don't understand it yourself." **Einstein**

"A clever person solves a problem. A wise person avoids it." **Einstein**

"Any fool can know. The point is to understand." **Einstein**

"I attribute the little I know to my not having been ashamed to ask for information, and to my rule of conversing with all descriptions of men on those topics that form their own peculiar professions and pursuits." **John Locke**

"The only fence against the world is a thorough knowledge of it." **John Locke**

"The improvement of understanding is for two ends: first, our own increase of knowledge; secondly, to enable us to deliver that knowledge to others. **John Locke**

"No man's knowledge here can go beyond his experience." **John Locke**

"Education and morals will be found almost the whole that goes to make a good man." **Aristotle**

"By three methods we may learn wisdom: First, by reflection, which is noblest; Second, by imitation, which is easiest; and third by experience, which is the bitterest." **Confucius**

"Education is the best provision for the journey to old age." **Aristotle**

"The roots of education are bitter, but the fruit is sweet." **Aristotle**

"The educated differ from the uneducated as much as the living from the dead." **Aristotle**

"Those who educate children well are more to be honored than they who produce them for these only gave them life, those the art of living well." **Aristotle**

"Beware the man of a single book."
Thomas Aquinas

"Misfortune seldom intrudes upon the wise man; his greatest and highest interests are directed by reason throughout the course of life."
Epicurus

"In order to improve the mind, we ought less to learn than to contemplate." **René Descartes**

"The reading of all good books is like conversation with the finest men of past centuries." **René Descartes**

"It is not enough to have a good mind; the main thing is to use it well."
René Descartes

"What we have to learn to do, we learn by doing." **Aristotle**

"For the things we have to learn before we can do them, we learn by doing them." **Aristotle**

"It is the mark of an educated mind to be able to entertain a thought without accepting it". **Aristotle**

"If you think in terms of a year, plant a seed if in terms of ten years, plant trees if in terms of years, teach the people" **Confucius**

"It is not possible for one to teach others who cannot teach his own family." **Confucius**

"A fool despises good counsel, but a wise man takes it to heart."
Confucius

"Only the wisest and the stupidest of men never change."
Confucius

"Learning without thought is labor lost. Thought without learning is perilous." **Confucius**

"Acquire new knowledge whilst thinking over the old, and you may become a teacher of others." **Confucius**

"Wisdom, compassion, and courage are the three universally recognized moral qualities of men." **Confucius**

Study the past if you would divine the future. **Confucius**

"The superior man acts before he speaks, and afterwards speaks according to his action." **Confucius**

"The important thing is not to stop questioning. Curiosity has its own reason for existing." **Einstein**

"Wise men talk because they have something to say; fools, because they have to say something." **Plato**

"You are young, my son, and, as the years go by, time will change and even reverse many of your present opinions. Refrain therefore awhile from setting yourself up as a judge of the highest matters". **Plato**

Deep doubts, deep wisdom; small doubts, small wisdom.
Chinese Proverb

There is no shame in not knowing; the shame lies in not finding out. - **Russian Proverb**

You're never too old to learn.

A spoon does not know the taste of soup, nor a learned fool the taste of wisdom. **Welsh Proverb**

A teacher is better than two books. **German Proverb**

Bible Verses on Education & Learning

Proverbs 1:5
A wise man will hear and increase in learning, And a man of understanding will acquire wise counsel,

Proverbs 1:7
The fear of the Lord is the beginning of knowledge;
Fools despise wisdom and instruction.

Proverbs 2:2
Make your ear attentive to wisdom,
Incline your heart to understanding;

Proverbs 2:6
For the Lord gives wisdom;
From His mouth come knowledge and understanding.

Proverbs 3:13
How blessed is the man who finds wisdom
And the man who gains understanding

Proverbs 9:9
Give instruction to a wise man and he will be still wiser, Teach a righteous man and he will increase his learning.

Proverbs 4:5
Acquire wisdom! Acquire understanding! Do not forget nor turn away from the words of my mouth.

Proverbs 8:11
"For wisdom is better than jewels; And all desirable things cannot compare with her.

Proverbs 4:7
"The beginning of wisdom is: Acquire wisdom; And with all your acquiring, get understanding.

Proverbs 9:10
The fear of the Lord is the beginning of wisdom, And the knowledge of the Holy One is understanding.

Proverbs 11:2
When pride comes, then comes dishonor, But with the humble is wisdom.

Proverbs 16:16
How much better it is to get wisdom than gold! And to get understanding is to be chosen above silver.

Proverbs 19:8
He who gets wisdom loves his own soul; He who keeps understanding will find good.

Proverbs 13:20
He who walks with wise men will be wise,
But the companion of fools will suffer harm.

James 3:17
But the wisdom from above is first pure, then peaceable, gentle, reasonable, full of mercy and good fruits, unwavering, without hypocrisy.

James 1:5
But if any of you lacks wisdom, let him ask of God, who gives to all generously and without reproach, and it will be given to him.

Job 12:12
"Wisdom is with aged men,
With long life is understanding.

Psalm 111:10
The fear of the Lord is the beginning of wisdom;
A good understanding have all those who do His commandments;
His praise endures forever.

Colossians 3:16
Let the word of Christ richly dwell within you, with all wisdom teaching and admonishing one another with psalms and hymns and spiritual songs, singing with thankfulness in your hearts to God.

Preparation, Procrastination and Perseverance

When it comes to planning and being prepared, I have my own saying: "have a plan and work your plan". This means you have to plan and prepare, but just as important, you must execute the plan as well. It is not enough to have a good plan without the time, energy or effort to implement and follow through on your plan.

There are many things in life we need to plan and prepare for. I have four children and it was important early in their life to plan and prepare for college expenses. We just assumed that all of our children would go to college and we would be 100% responsible for all of the expenses. We did not hope or dream of scholarships or a rich uncle to die and leave us money. You see, HOPE is not a strategy or plan. We can hope for the best, but we plan for the worst!!

Obviously this book cannot delineate all the things to plan and prepare for, so included in this chapter is a few of the more important things that I believe you should plan and prepare for.

Procrastination is the opposite of planning and preparation. I hate procrastination with a passion. It just lets problems fester and puts off the day of reckoning. Better to deal with the issue and problem right away, it usually does not get better.

Perseverance - My grandfather would have called this "stick-to-itiveness". To keep going when you want to quit or stop. How easy it is to quit and not complete your tasks.   This is a character trait you want to develop and hone in your life and the life of your family.   You will need to model this behavior for your children so they can see what it takes to keep going in the face of obstacles and adversity.

I still remember the time when my oldest daughter was competing in a cheerleading competition and she was very ill.   They had competed the first day and she was fine, but on the final day she got very sick. She wanted to quit and asked my advice.   I knew their routine was only a couple of minutes long - so this is what I said:

"I believe in you and you can do anything for 2 1/2 minutes. Now go do you best"

She went on to perform the event and absolutely nailed the last stunt that none of the other girls were willing to try (they feared failing in public - even though some of them were actually better in practice).

That was many years ago, and to this day she and I will reference that time when she is facing difficulty.

It will be critical for you to encourage others when they face obstacles and adversity and at times to stand in the gap with them.

It is always too soon to quit

Quitting is always the easy choice. Choose to stick with it just a little while longer.   If necessary just get by minute by minute or day by day.

Manage you time - rich, poor, strong or weak, we all only have 24 hours each day -

To many people stumble through life not thinking about the time that is lost each day.   Once a day is gone, it cannot be redeemed.   It does not matter who you are in life, we all only get 24 hours each day. How you choose to use those hours will set in motion how much you will accomplish.

At a minimum, have a will

Having a will is so critical for every married couple. This is especially true if you have children. If you don't want your crazy Aunt Lizzy raising your children if you were both to die, then you better have a will that states exactly who will raise your children.

Have other medical and end of life documents ready

Nobody wants to think about getting sick, being incapacitated, death and dying. It is a morbid subject and not a subject most people want to broach. However, it is better to be prepared and avoid some difficult decisions when you will most likely be overwhelmed.

I will not go into great detail here, but would advise you to do additional research to better understand all of these components:

- Durable power of attorney - for others to manage your finances

- Health care power of attorney, or health care proxy -for others to direct your health care.

- Medical-information release - This lets others get access to your medical records.

- Living will/Advanced Health Care Directive. - Tells others the kind of treatment you want.

You will need to execute these documents ahead of time. I would advise meeting with a lawyer who specializes in this area to guide and direct you.

Buy term life insurance for your family's sake

The whole point on life insurance is that you never get it use it! Life insurance is for the loved ones you leave behind. The usual recommendation is 10 times your salary. You want your family to be able to continue life as comfortably as possible if you were to pass away. The reason for Term life insurance is that if offers the greatest coverage for the least cost. Forget getting any other type of life insurance and stick with term life.

Buy an umbrella insurance policy to cover you

An umbrella policy covers you above and beyond where your other insurance coverage ends. Think of it this way - if you were to cause a 5 car accident, most likely your auto insurance would not cover all of the risk. With the umbrella policy, it helps protect your assets. Considering how much coverage you get, it is a wise investment.

An ounce of prevention is worth a pound of cure

This is a very old saying. It is better to get your flu shot early in the season and avoid getting the flu. It might cost you $25 to get the flu shot, but if you get the flu it could cost you a week of work and ton of money. Not to mention the cost of the medicine and doctor visit to get over the flu.

Do the hard task first

It is easy to do the easy task first, because they are easy. Some people follow this philosophy and never get to the hard tasks. I have found it better to accomplish the hard tasks first - especially while I am fresh and have the energy to complete them. It I waited to do the hard tasks last, then I find that I am tired and weary and distracted from all the easy and small tasks.

Always read the instructions

Men are notorious for not reading directions or instructions. We think we can save time and just "wing it". I have been guilty of this too many times. I have found that I actually save time, energy and effort by reading the instructions.

Always put the big rocks in the jar first

If you have a jar and a large group of rocks, if you want to get then all in the jar, then you have to put the large rocks in first. If you put in the small rocks first, then there will not be room for the large rocks. So what does this mean? What this means is that you need to take care of the big things in life first and get them done before you do the small things. It also literally means sometimes to put the big things in first. Whenever we pack to go camping, we also pack the van with the largest things (which also happen to be some of the most important things), we then fill in the gaps and spaces with the smaller items.

Be prepared

Being prepared means to think through the situations coming up in life that you can plan for ahead of time. We learned this as we would go hiking and backpacking in the woods. There are no resources other than those that you bring with you into the woods. We never stepped into the woods without the following:

- Knife
- Whistle
- Flashlight
- Way to Start a fire - lighter, matches and tinder
- Compass and Map

The whole point of always having these few items is that you were setting yourself up for success if you ever got lost. You had a way to stay warm, purify water, signal rescuers, and make a shelter.

We had one of our boys get lost on a hiking trip and he had all of his equipment and followed our plan. When he realized he was lost, he stopped and hugged a tree and started blowing his whistle. We were able to quickly find him because he was prepared.

Being prepared means you have to be intentional and have forethought of your actions and plans.

Here are some things that generally affect everyone. Are you prepared?

- Death
- Loss of employment
- Injury or accident
- School/College expense
- Storms (hurricane, blizzard, tornado, flood, etc.)
- Fire
- Mechanical breakdown
- Lost

These are just a few common "risks" we have in life. Being prepared means that you are effectively managing the risk so as to minimize your loss.

Have goals for life and write them down

They say that a goal is not real until you write it down. I have found this to be very true. If you really want to make a commitment to these goals, then have others hold you accountable to them.

If you are going to have goals - make them SMART goals

I am a huge believer in goals and goal setting. I believe that you must write you goals down and be accountable to someone if you really want to achieve them.

The best method I have found is SMART goals. S.M.A.R.T goals means, Specific, Measurable, Actionable, Reasonable and Time Bound.

I want to juxtapose examples of non-smart goals and SMART goals. We will assume this family makes $60,000 per year and has one son who is 8 years old

Non-smart goal

"We want to save money for college."

While this may sound good, it is too vague, not measurable, not time-bound.

SMART goal

"We want to save $20,000 over the next 10 years for our son's college expenses. We will save $167 each month starting next month and invest the money in a 529 savings plan."

This goal meets all of the criteria to be a SMART goal

Specific – Money for son's college into a 529 plan

Measurable - $20,000 (or $167 each month)

Actionable – start next month

Reasonable – on a monthly basis this is about 3.3% of their income.

Time-bound – each month for the next 10 years

This was a fairly easy example of a financial goal, but goal setting can be used in every aspect of your life – spiritual, financial, relational, emotional and physical.   Using goals and goal setting is a way of life and is a learned skill.   Just because you never used goals before is not an excuse for not using them now.

Never put off until tomorrow, what you can do today

It may seem good to put off a task for the next day, but if you can do it today, it is better to get it done.   The main reason for this is that you do not know what tomorrow will bring!   This happens at work all the time.   You have time to complete a task early and get it out of the way today, but you put it off. Unfortunately, the next day your boss gives you a new set of tasks or priorities or an emergency comes up and you do not get the task completed.

I have also seen this happen with my children on college assignments. They are given a deadline to complete and post an assignment and they think they can wait until the last minute to complete it.   What happens if you lose power and the internet goes down?? Then you cannot complete the assignment.   This actually happened.   I tried to tell them to complete it early, but they did not listen to me.   I was working on my MBA during this time and had similar assignments and did complete mine early and did not have any issues.   I was able to share this as a very practical learning lesson with them.

Have a "bolt bag" ready

If you live in an area of the country that is prone to natural disaster - earthquakes or hurricanes, then it is a good idea to have a bolt bag ready to go.   This is just a bag that has the basic necessities of life for you to get by for a couple of day.

Below is what the American Red Cross Suggests you should have to be prepared: (Source: Redcross.org)

At a minimum, you should have the basic supplies listed below:

- Water: one gallon per person, per day (3-day supply for evacuation, 2-week supply for home)
- Food: non-perishable, easy-to-prepare items (3-day supply for evacuation, 2-week supply for home)
- Flashlight

- Battery-powered or hand-crank radio (NOAA Weather Radio, if possible)
- Extra batteries
- First aid kit
- Medications (7-day supply) and medical items
- Multi-purpose tool
- Sanitation and personal hygiene items
- Copies of personal documents (medication list and pertinent medical information, proof of address, deed/lease to home, passports, birth certificates, insurance policies)
- Cell phone with chargers
- Family and emergency contact information
- Extra cash
- Emergency blanket
- Map(s) of the area
- Consider the needs of all family members and add supplies to your kit.

Suggested items to help meet additional needs are:

- Medical supplies (hearing aids with extra batteries, glasses, contact lenses, syringes, etc)
- Baby supplies (bottles, formula, baby food, diapers)
- Games and activities for children
- Pet supplies (collar, leash, ID, food, carrier, bowl)
- Two-way radios
- Extra set of car keys and house keys
- Manual can opener

Additional supplies to keep at home or in your survival kit based on the types of disasters common to your area:

- Whistle
- N95 or surgical masks
- Matches
- Rain gear
- Towels
- Work gloves
- Tools/supplies for securing your home
- Extra clothing, hat and sturdy shoes

- Plastic sheeting
- Duct tape
- Scissors
- Household liquid bleach
- Entertainment items
- Blankets or sleeping bags

Use the Red Cross website to help prepare a plan for emergencies

The Red Cross web site is a great resource for creating a plan and checklist for all types of major disasters.

Attitude is everything

You cannot always choose your circumstances, but you can always choose your attitude. Choose to stick it out and go the extra mile.

Surround yourself with positive people who will encourage you

To persevere, it is important to surround yourself with family and friends who will speak encouragement into your life and sometimes even come along side you. Avoid the whiners and nay sayers. They do not have your best interest in mind.

Quotes on Preparation, Procrastination and Perseverance

"You may delay, but time will not." **Ben Franklin**

"Delay not to seize the hour!" **Aeschylus**

"I never knew a man who was good at making excuses who was good at anything else." **Ben Franklin**

"This one makes a net, this one stands and wishes. Would you like to make a bet which one gets the fishes." **Chinese Rhyme**

"By failing to prepare you are preparing to fail." **Ben Franklin**

"The best way to get something done is to begin." **Unknown**

"If and When were planted, and Nothing grew." **Unknown**

"Procrastination is the thief of time." **Edward Young**

"If you put off everything till you're sure of it, you'll never get anything done." **Norman Vincent Peale**

"Begin to weave and God will give you the thread." **German Proverb**

"When there is a hill to climb, don't think that waiting will make it smaller." **Unknown**

"Procrastination is the grave in which opportunity is buried." **Unknown**

"Things may come to those who wait, but only the things left by those who hustle." **Abraham Lincoln**

"One of these days, is none of these days." **Unknown**

"You don't have to see the whole staircase, just take the first step." **Martin Luther King, Jr.**

"The only difference between success and failure is the ability to take action." **Alexandre Graham Bell**

"You cannot plough a field by turning it over in your mind." **Unknown**

"Don't wait. The time will never be just right." **Napoleon Hill**

"You cannot escape the responsibility of tomorrow by evading it today." **Abraham Lincoln**

"The two rules of procrastination: 1) Do it today. 2) Tomorrow will be today tomorrow." **Unknown**

"What may be done at any time will be done at no time." **Scottish Proverb**

"Tomorrow is often the busiest day of the week." **Spanish Proverb**

"Neither a wise nor a brave man lies down on the tracks of history to wait for the train of the future to run over him." **Dwight D. Eisenhower**

"Whatever you want to do, do it now! There are only so many tomorrows." **Michael Landon**

"My advice is to never do tomorrow what you can do today. Procrastination is the thief of time." **Charles Dickens**

"A man who does not think and plan long ahead will find trouble right at his door." **Confucius**

"Well begun is half done." **Aristotle**

"Our greatest glory is not in never falling, but in rising every time we fall." **Confucius**

"It's always too early to quit." **Norman Vincent Peale**

"Winners never quit and quitters never win." **Vince Lombardi**

"If you believe in yourself and have dedication and pride - and never quit, you'll be a winner. The price of victory is high but so are the rewards." **Paul Bryant**

"Age wrinkles the body. Quitting wrinkles the soul."
Douglas MacArthur

"Patience and perseverance have a magical effect before which difficulties disappear and obstacles vanish." **John Quincy Adams**

"Perseverance is the hard work you do after you get tired of doing the hard work you already did." **Newt Gingrich**

Fall seven times and stand up eight. **Japanese Proverb**

"It's not that I'm so smart; it's just that I stay with problems longer."
Albert Einstein

"Many of life's failures are people who did not realize how close they were to success when they gave up." **Thomas Edison**

"Failure is only the opportunity to begin again, this time more intelligently." **Henry Ford**

"It does not matter how slowly you go so long as you do not stop."
Confucius

"Never confuse a single defeat with a final defeat." **F. Scott Fitzgerald**

"Perseverance is failing 19 times and succeeding the 20th".
Julie Andrews

"Through perseverance many people win success out of what seemed destined to be certain failure. " **Ben Disraeli**

"Success seems to be largely a matter of hanging on after others have let go". **William Feather**

"Develop success from failures. Discouragement and failure are two of the surest stepping stones to success. " **Dale Carnegie**

"We will either find a way or make one." **Hannibal**

"It always seems impossible until it's done". **Nelson Mandela**

"A winner is just a loser who tried one more time"
George M. Moore Jr.

" Defeat is not the worst of failures. Not to have tried is the true failure" **George Edward Woodberry**

"When you get into a tight place and everything goes against you … never give up then, for that is just the place and time that the tide will turn." **Harriet Beecher Stowe**

"The man who moves a mountain begins by carrying away small stones." **Confucius**

"I am a slow walker, but I never walk back". **Abraham Lincoln**

"Every strike brings me closer to the next home run." **Babe Ruth**

"Courage is not having the strength to go on; it is going on when you don't have the strength." **Theodore Roosevelt**

"Character consists of what you do on the third and fourth tries."
James A. Michener

"Perseverance is not a long race; it is many short races one after the other." **Walter Elliot**

"I was taught the way of progress is neither swift nor easy."
Marie Curie

"If you are going through hell, keep going." **Winston Churchill**

"Never quit. It is the easiest cop-out in the world. Set a goal and don't quit until you attain it. When you do attain it, set another goal, and don't quit until you reach it. Never quit."
Bear Bryant

"Never, never, never give up". **Winston Churchill**

"The harder you work, the harder it is to surrender."
Vince Lombardi

"He is a man of courage who does not run away, but remains at his post and fights against the enemy." **Socrates**

"Conquer yourself rather than the world." **René Descartes**

"I count him braver who overcomes his desires than him who overcomes his enemies." **Aristotle**

"He who conquers himself is the mightiest warrior" **Confucius**

"The gem cannot be polished without friction nor man without trials."
Confucius

"The superior man will watch over himself when he is alone. He examines his heart that there may be nothing wrong there, and that he may have no cause of dissatisfaction with himself." **Confucius**

"It's not whether you get knocked down, it's whether you get up."
Vince Lombardi

"Once you learn to quit, it becomes a habit." **Vince Lombardi**

"Obstacles are what you see when you take your eyes off of the goal."
- **Vince Lombardi**

"You never fail until you stop trying." **Einstein**

Fall seven times, stand up eight. **Japanese Proverb**

If at first you don't succeed, try, try again.

"Industry, perseverance & frugality make fortune yield." **Ben Franklin**

"You cannot escape the responsibility of tomorrow by evading it today." **Abraham Lincoln**

Bible Verses on Preparation, Procrastination and Perseverance

Proverbs 6:6-8
Go to the ant, O sluggard,
Observe her ways and be wise,
Which, having no chief,
Officer or ruler,
Prepares her food in the summer
And gathers her provision in the harvest

Proverbs 12:24
The hand of the diligent will rule,
But the slack hand will be put to forced labor.

Proverbs 13:4
The soul of the sluggard craves and gets nothing,
But the soul of the diligent is made fat.

Proverbs 20:4
The sluggard does not plow after the autumn,
So he begs during the harvest and has nothing.

Proverbs 27:1
Do not boast about tomorrow,
For you do not know what a day may bring forth.

Luke 12:40
You too, be ready; for the Son of Man is coming at an hour that you do not expect."

Proverbs 20:13
Do not love sleep, or you will become poor;
Open your eyes, and you will be satisfied with food.

Proverbs 10:4
Poor is he, who works with a negligent hand,
But the hand of the diligent makes rich.

Proverbs 12:27
A lazy man does not roast his prey,
But the precious possession of a man is diligence.

Proverbs 22:3
The prudent sees the evil and hides himself,
But the simple go on, and are punished for it.

Proverbs 27:12
A prudent man sees evil and hides himself,
The simple proceed and pay the penalty.

Romans 15:4-6
For whatever was written in earlier times was written for our instruction, so that through perseverance and the encouragement of the Scriptures we might have hope. Now may the God who gives perseverance and encouragement grant you to be of the same mind with one another according to Christ Jesus, so that with one accord you may with one voice glorify the God and Father of our Lord Jesus Christ.

Romans 5:3-5
And not only this, but we also exult in our tribulations, knowing that tribulation brings about perseverance; and perseverance, proven character; and proven character, hope; and hope does not disappoint, because the love of God has been poured out within our hearts through the Holy Spirit who was given to us.

James 1:12
Blessed is a man who perseveres under trial; for once he has been approved, he will receive the crown of life which the Lord has promised to those who love Him.

Galatians 6:9
Let us not lose heart in doing good, for in due time we will reap if we do not grow weary.

2 Thessalonians 3:13
But as for you, brethren, do not grow weary of doing good.

James 1:2-4

Consider it all joy, my brethren, when you encounter various trials, 3 knowing that the testing of your faith produces endurance. 4 And let endurance have its perfect result, so that you may be perfect and complete, lacking in nothing.

Health

You only get one body to travel through this life with. It is better to make the early investment in taking care of your body so that you can lead a long and productive life. You will also want to be as useful as you can for as long as you can - not only for your sake, but for those who depend on you as well.

Get up from your chair every hour and walk around

Many of us have jobs these days that require us to sit behind a desk. If that is your lot in life, then set your alarm for every hour and get up and walk around. Stretch a little and if possible even go outside for a breath of fresh air.

Make exercise part of your daily routine

Make this priority in your life. It will require sacrifice and effort, but it is an excellent habit to start when you are young.   I am older now and I will tell you that it is much harder and takes more effort these days, but I am very glad this has been a life long habit.

It means I have to get up at 5:00 am some days to get the exercise in, but for me it is a very effective stress reliever with the obvious health benefits.

Over 50, have a colonoscopy

I have had several good friends over 50 who had colorectal cancer detected early because of this advice.

Get an annual physical

This is just good common sense! Just do it.

Regularly get tested for breast cancer for woman and prostate cancer for men

This is just good common sense! Just do it. There is a certain age and time depending on many factors, so you will want to check with you doctor and find out the best time to start testing.

For my bride, her mother and grandmother and aunt all had breast cancer. You had better believe that we have been having these tests on a regular basis.

Get your teeth cleaned twice per year

Basic maintenance on your teeth will pay huge dividends in the long run. It is a small sacrifice in time to prevent future problems - that almost always cost a lot more money and time.

Brush your teeth between meals

Also brush your teeth in the morning and before you go to bed. This goes along with the advice above. In addition, those who are nearest to you will greatly appreciate it.

Wear sun screen or use an umbrella or protective clothing

Ask my bride about the skin cancer she has from the younger years of not having any skin protection and spending too much time in the sun. We know so much more these days about the damaging effects of too much sun. Don't avoid the great outdoors, just protect you skin and your exposure

Don't Smoke

Duh!!! I cannot believe that anybody in this day and age still smokes. We have more than enough evidence to prove the harm that it does to your body.

Find a good dentist and doctor

Ask your friends, family and neighbors for recommendations for a good doctor and dentist. These are long term relationships you want to build, so take the time to find someone who is competent and who you trust.

Do not consume adult beverages

I should say Duh here as well, but I know that I am in the minority in this opinion. However, I would just say two things:

1. You have a **ZERO** percent chance of becoming an alcoholic if you never drink adult beverages.

2. You have ZERO percent chance of making a foolish decision or choice while you are impaired by alcohol. Such as driving or saying or doing something you would not otherwise do.

People will tell you that it is ok to drink in moderation. I say baloney. Don't drink at all. Do not do it, do not start.

I will also say from a budget stand point, you will save a ton of money!

Protect what goes into your eyes and ears - be very thoughtful

This is a warning against all the trash and filth that is available on the internet. Pornography is such a powerful evil because it is addictive and the images never leave your mind. They are seared into your memory to be brought up in moments of weakness and anger. I can promise you from personal experience that you do not want to go down this path. Find someone to hold you accountable and get the proper software loaded on your computer.

Tattoos really are forever

Think carefully about how it will look in 50 years. It may seem very cool today, but will you think it is cool when you are 60 years old? I wish every tattoo parlor had a website that would "age you" and show you what you will look like in the future. I have never regretted not getting a tattoo.

Wear a helmet

If a helmet is suggested, then wear it! This could be for a work site, bike ride, climbing or motorcycle ride. Better safe than sorry.

Recognize the most stressful activities and how they affect you

Below is the Holmes and Rahe Stress Scale, that list the 35 most stressful activities. Take a moment to see how many of these are in your life right now. You can also take a test on Stress.org to find out your total score. Knowing they key triggers to stress and how much stress you are really under can help you start to effectively deal with it.

	(score)
1. Death of spouse	(100)
2. Divorce	(73)
3. Marital separation	(65)
4. Jail term	(63)
5. Death of close family member	(63)
6. Personal injury or illness	(53)
7. Marriage (getting married)	(50)
8. Fired at work	(47)
9. Marital reconciliation	(45)
10. Retirement	(45)
11. Change in health of family member	(44)
12. Pregnancy	(40)
13. Sex difficulties	(39)
14. Gain of new family member	(39)
15. Business readjustment	(39)
16. Change in financial state	(38)
17. Death of close friend	(37)
18. Change to a different line of work	(36)
19. Change in number of arguments with spouse	(35)
20. A large mortgage or loan	(31)
21. Foreclosure of mortgage or loan	(30)
22. Change in responsibilities at work	(29)
23. Son or daughter leaving home	(29)
24. Trouble with in-laws	(29)
25. Outstanding personal achievement	(28)
26. Spouse begins or stops work	(26)
27. Begin or end school/college	(26)
28. Change in living conditions	(25)
29. Revision of personal habits	(24)
30. Trouble with boss	(23)
31. Change in work hours or conditions	(20)
32. Change in residence	(20)
33. Change in school/college	(20)
34. Change in recreation	(19)
35. Change in church activities	(19)

Also, knowing these scores and triggers will help you deal with others who are going through difficulty in their life.

Make joy and laughter a part of each day

Laughter relaxes the body and reduces stress. Look for ways to laugh at yourself and with and others

Eat more fruits and vegetables

Yes your grandmother was right when she told you to eat more fruits and vegetables. They are good for you and full of vitamins and minerals.

Learn to get 7-8 hours of sleep each night

They have done many studies that show the minimum amount of sleep needed for an adult is 7-8 hours per night. Do not stress your body by not getting sleep and rest.

Do not skip breakfast, it is the most important meal of the day

Start your day right with a healthy, well balanced breakfast.

.

Quotes on Health

"A sound mind in a sound body, is a short, but full description of a happy state in this World: he that has these two, has little more to wish for; and he that wants either of them, will be little the better for anything else." **John Locke**

"Early to bed and early to rise makes a man healthy, wealthy and wise." **Ben Franklin**

"The greatest wealth is Health." **Unknown**

"Let food be thy medicine and medicine be thy food" **Hippocrates**

"Just because you're not sick doesn't mean you're healthy" **Unknown**

"If you don't take care of your body, where are you going to live?" **Unknown**

"Health is like money, we never have a true idea of its value until we lose it." **Josh Billings**

"Take care of your body. It's the only place you have to live." **Jim Rohn**

The more you eat, the less flavor; the less you eat, the more flavor. **Chinese Proverb**

A man too busy to take care of his health is like a mechanic too busy to take care of his tools. **Spanish Proverb**

"The part can never be well unless the whole is well." **Plato**

"Walking is man's best medicine." **Hippocrates**

"An apple a day keeps the doctor away." **Unknown**

"Physical fitness is not only one of the most important keys to a healthy body, it is the basis of dynamic and creative intellectual activity." **John F. Kennedy**

"The only way to keep your health is to eat what you don't want, drink what you don't like, and do what you'd rather not." **Mark Twain**

"To keep the body in good health is a duty, otherwise we shall not be able to keep our mind strong and clear." **Buddha**

"Lack of activity destroys the good condition of every human being, while movement and methodical physical exercise save it and preserve it." **Plato**

"The greatest wealth is health." **Virgil**

"He who takes medicine and neglects to diet wastes the skill of his doctors." **Chinese Proverb**

"A good laugh and a long sleep are the best cures in the doctor's book." **Irish Proverb**

"Health is the greatest gift, contentment the greatest wealth, faithfulness the best relationship" **Buddha**

"Attention to health is life's greatest hindrance." **Plato**

"Our bodies are our gardens – our wills are our gardeners." **Shakespeare**

The more you eat, the less flavor; the less you eat, the more flavor. **Chinese Proverb**

"The part can never be well unless the whole is well". **Plato**

Fresh air impoverishes the doctor. **Danish Proverb**

"It is wonderful how the mind is stirred and quickened into activity by brisk bodily exercise." **Pliny The Younger**

"If the body be feeble, the mind will not be strong." **Thomas Jefferson**

"It is exercise alone that supports the spirits, and keeps the mind in vigor" **Cicero**

"Lack of activity destroys the good condition of every human being, while movement and methodical physical exercise save it and preserve it." **Plato**

"When it comes to health, diet is the Queen, but exercise is the King."
Jack Lalanne

The best six doctors anywhere
And no one can deny it
Are sunshine, water, rest, and air
Exercise and diet.
These six will gladly you attend
If only you are willing
Your mind they'll ease
Your will they'll mend
And charge you not a shilling.
– Nursery rhyme

Bible Verses on Health

1 Corinthians 6:19-20
Or do you not know that your body is a temple of the Holy Spirit who is in you, whom you have from God, and that you are not your own? For you have been bought with a price: therefore glorify God in your body.

Romans 12:1-2
Therefore I urge you, brethren, by the mercies of God, to present your bodies a living and holy sacrifice, acceptable to God, which is your spiritual service of worship. 2 And do not be conformed to this world, but be transformed by the renewing of your mind, so that you may prove what the will of God is, that which is good and acceptable and perfect.

1 Corinthians 10:31
Whether, then, you eat or drink or whatever you do, do all to the glory of God.

1 Timothy 4:8
for bodily discipline is only of little profit, but godliness is profitable for all things, since it holds promise for the present life and also for the life to come.

1 Corinthians 9:24-27
Do you not know that those who run in a race all run, but only one receives the prize? Run in such a way that you may win. Everyone who competes in the games exercises self-control in all things. They then do it to receive a perishable wreath, but we an imperishable. Therefore I run in such a way, as not without aim; I box in such a way, as not beating the air; but I discipline my body and make it my slave, so that, after I have preached to others, I myself will not be disqualified

Cars/Driving & Traveling

Everybody looks forward to turning 16 years old and getting behind the wheel of their first car. It is an exciting time and offers the chance for freedom and independence. However, we tend to forget that a car is basically a 2,000 lb. missile that can cause incredible damage and destruction if not used properly. In addition, for most people the second biggest expense they have after their house is their car.

Learning to be a safe driver and taking care of your investment is a good use of your time, energy and effort.

Traveling in your own country and around the world is a wonderful and exciting thing to do. It expands you understanding of other cultures and exposes you to the beauty of the world. Take the opportunity to explore - especially while you are young.

Read the Owner's Manual for your car

You will be absolutely surprised at what you find in the owner's manual. It is a great reference book and contains great information on issues and solutions.

Change the oil in your car often

Do this every 3,000 to 5,000 miles to extend the life of your car. Follow the advice in the owner manual. Don't forget to change the air filter every 12,000 - 15,000 miles as well.

Be prepared for emergencies

Always keep 50 feet of rope, jumper cables, various tools, flashlight and water in your trunk. In the winter, keep a blanket, boots, shovel, a hat and extra cloths in your trunk.

AAA is great peace of mind

We have had AAA for a long time and we use it at least once a year for a tow or other roadside issue.   We do drive older cars, so the peace of mind is real and very comforting.   In addition, we get great travel books, maps, discounts and auto repair recommendations when out of town.

Learn to do the basic maintenance on your car:

Change your own oil
Change your own brake pads
Change you own transmission fluid

There are so many great videos on the internet to show you how easy it is to do all these things.

Follow the maintenance schedule for your car

It will cost you a little money upfront to do this, but will save you from breakdowns and expensive repairs.   It will also extend the life of your car.

Have a spare key for your motor vehicles

Each member of our family has spare keys to each other's cars. This has proven very helpful on many occasions.   You should also consider keeping a spare key in a magnet box under the wheel well.

Find a good mechanic

This can be tough, as there are many incompetent and dishonest mechanics out there.   Use your social network to find a good one and keep them!   A good mechanic is worth their weight in gold

Do not text and drive

Distracted driving is the number one cause of accidents these days. Arrive alive! That text can wait

Do not drive impaired

This means do not drink and drive or do drugs and drive.

Do not buy your children a car- make them earn it

Make them earn it! Everybody needs to have "skin in the game". There is nothing like ownership that brings with it the desire to take care of the investment and treat it properly.

With my children what we did was institute the "Dad savings plan". With this plan I matched their savings dollar for dollar for every dollar they saved for their car. In addition, we also required them to have $1,000 saving for repairs and emergencies as well as paying for their auto insurance.

How did they do it? They got jobs and worked their tails off! No free lunches in our house. They could also earn bonuses for good grades when they go to college. Making Dean's list would pay for their auto insurance for 6 month (no small amount of money) and Presidents list was a $500 additional bonus on top of the Dean's list bonus. This was pretty good motivation for them to do well.

Pay cash for a good used car - have money in bank for repairs -

There is nothing more useless than making a payment on a depreciating asset. Cars only go down in value. Consider only buying cars that are at least 7 to 8 years old. They have typically depreciated 75% to 80% by that time and you can still find really good cars in that age range. This means you could buy a $30,000 car for about $7,000. I actually buy cars that are about 12 years old and have saved a ton of money.

Be most careful when you back up

Most accidents happen when you are backing up. So be sure to slow down, take your time and look around before you back up.

Do not drive is you are sleepy or drowsy

Either do not start the journey and get some rest first, or pull over and get some rest.

Always wear your seatbelt

You never know when an accident is going to happen, so better safe than sorry. Be a good example to your children and always wear your seat belt.

Do not follow too closely

The rule of thumb is to allow a three second gap between you and the car in front of you. At night or in bad weather you should double this time.

Never let your gas gauge get below 1/4 tank full

Even better, do not let it get below 1/2 full if possible. Running out of can be very dangerous and at a minimum it is a huge inconvenience.

Be more careful when driving in the Rain, Snow or Fog

You will want to slow down and allow more time for travel. Do not follow the cars in front of you as closely. Give yourself more time and distance to stop. Invest in snow tires and chains as a means to stay safe during wintery weather.

Do not put all your trust in the GPS systems

Keep old fashion maps in your car. The GPS is not always up to date and has been known to be very wrong. AAA has excellent maps that are free with membership. Before long car trips, I always stop by their office and get maps (or you can also order them over the internet).

Don't just use your mirrors when changing lanes

Physically turn and look. There is a blind spot. We live in a very large metro area and this has saved me more times than I can tell you. I look in the mirror and everything seems fine, and then I turn to look and sure enough a car or motorcycle is there.

Don't stop for flashing lights behind you in a deserted area

Keep driving until you get to a safe area and do not be afraid to call 911 to confirm you are being pulled over by a real police officer.

A green light does not mean go at once!

If you are first in line at a stop light, always wait a second or two before going when the light turns green. This may annoy the people behind you, but too many times I have had some fool fly through the intersection after his light has turned red.

When we lived in Texas someone told me this saying: "Green means Go - Yellow means speed up - Red means three more cars"

Use Kelly Blue Book and Edmunds to determine car values

These are two really good resources for you to find out how much a used car is worth.

Have a really good checklist when you go to buy a used car

I actually have a four page checklist that I use to evaluate a used car. I look at the interior, exterior, engine and trunk. For each of those areas, I have a specific list of things to check. I also always take a test drive and make sure to check reverse! Here are 10 easy things to check that do not require any expertise:

- Lights (blinkers as well as brake lights)
- Windshield wipers
- Emergency flashers
- Heat and air conditioner
- Radio and CD player (bring a CD)
- Roll down all the widows
- Check to make sure all the doors open and lock
- Adjust all the seats
- Make sure there is a spare tire and tools to change it.
- Check glove box for owner's manual

Obviously these are the easy things to check, and you will ultimately want to check the engine and transmission as well.

Hire a mechanic to check a used car for you

If you are not comfortable checking out a used car, then just hire a mechanic to do this for you. It does not cost that much money and can give you peace of mind.

Always take a Carry-on Bag

When flying - ALWAYS take a carry-on bag with at least 1-2 days change of clothing and other key medical items. My favorite story is when we had a group of 100 kids and I told them all to follow this rule. Only one girl did. And sure enough, all of the luggage was delayed by two days. She thanked profusely because she was good to go.

Only pack as much as you want to carry

You can almost always buy what you need at your destination. Never take more than two bags - ever! Try to get by with a small backpack/large purse and a carryon roller bag.

Key Things to pack in your carry-on bag:

- All your money, passport, id and valuables
- Ear plugs
- All of your electronics (phone, computer, tablet, camera etc.)
- Cords and plugs for all of your electronics
- Bandana
- Small First Aid Kit
- Good water bottle
- Small roll of toilet paper and cleaning wipes
- Extra change of clothes to include underwear and socks
- Your small bag of liquids - toothpaste, shampoo, etc.
- Pen or pencil
- Your favorite comfort food snack
- Something to read - either a real book or e-book

Assume the airlines are going to lose or delay your checked bags. If you use that mentality then you will always be prepared for your trip.

Take lots of pictures

With digital cameras and phones you can always delete what you do not like or need. My bride and I took over 6,000 pictures on our anniversary trip to Italy (about 3,000 each) and we were surprised at the pictures we each took. She captured things I missed and vice versa. Be sure to capture people you know in as many of the pictures as possible. That is the thing you will most remember and want to cherish.

Carry extra cash

Cash is king in most countries outside the USA. I have found that US currency is almost universally accepted. Keep small bills $5, $10, $20

When traveling bring at least one comfort snack food from home

There is just something nice about having that one kind of snack you cannot get anywhere else. Outside the USA I have found that to be peanut butter.

Make copies of everything and leave with someone at home

This means copies of your travel itinerary, passport and other key documents. Some people take pictures or scan and save on their phone or computer. I am not convinced that is fool proof, but it is another backup idea.

A money belt is a great investment!

You can keep your passport and other documents completely safe from pick pockets. A money belt offers great peace of mind when traveling.

Take an extra battery pack that will charge your electronics!

This is probably one of the best things I did a couple of years ago. I have a large Limefuel battery pack that lets me charge my electronics for hours and hours!! It is a wonderful. I have never run out of battery power in a day and at right it has even powered a mini USB fan that provides ambient noise for sleeping.

Invest in a good guidebook

We have used Rick Steve's guidebooks and they are invaluable. They save time, money and point out things to avoid and things not to miss. There are many guidebooks to choose from, so just choose one you are most comfortable with.

Use the Internet to do your research before you go

I am a big believer in Trip Advisor®, Yelp®, Urban Spoon® and other websites that can help you prepare for your trip.

Try not to travel alone

There is safety in numbers and you will want to share the experience with someone else.

Eat like the locals

Ask the locals for food recommendations and try many different things. We have found "street food" to be some of the best food we eat. No need for a 5 star restaurant.

Quotes on Cars/Driving &Traveling

"We travel not to escape life, but for life not to escape us." Anonymous

"For my part, I travel not to go anywhere, but to go. I travel for travel's sake. The great affair is to move." Robert Louis Stevenson

"Adventure is worthwhile." Aristotle

"Broad, wholesome, charitable views of men and things cannot be acquired by vegetating in one little corner of the earth all of one's lifetime." Mark Twain

"The world is a book, and those who do not travel read only one page." – Saint Augustine

"Travel is fatal to prejudice, bigotry, and narrow-mindedness." Mark Twain

"He who does not travel does not know the value of men." Moorish proverb

"Travel is the only thing you buy that makes you richer." Unknown

"He who is outside his door has the hardest part of his journey behind him." Dutch Proverb

"It takes 8,460 bolts to assemble an automobile, and one nut to scatter it all over the road." Unknown

"A pedestrian is someone who thought there were a couple of gallons left in the tank." Unknown

"Never drive faster than your guardian angel can fly." Unknown

"When buying a used car, punch the buttons on the radio. If all the stations are rock and roll, there's a good chance the transmission is shot." Larry Lujack

"Another way to solve the traffic problems of this country is to pass a law that only paid-for cars be allowed to use the highways." Will Rogers

"A journey of a thousand miles must begin with a single step." Lao Tzu

"If you reject the food, ignore the customs, fear the religion and avoid the people, you might better stay at home." James Michener

"I shall be telling this with a sigh somewhere ages and ages hence: Two roads diverged in a wood, and I – I took the one less traveled by, and that has made all the difference." Robert Frost

"Travel, in the younger sort, is a part of education; in the elder, a part of experience." Francis Bacon

"Experience, travel – these are as education in themselves" Euripides

"When preparing to travel, lay out all your clothes and all your money. Then take half the clothes and twice the money." Susan Heller

"A man of ordinary talent will always be ordinary, whether he travels or not; but a man of superior talent will go to pieces if he remains forever in the same place...." Wolfgang Amadeus Mozart

"People who don't travel cannot have a global view, all they see is what's in front of them. Those people cannot accept new things because all they know is where they live." Martin Yan

"Travel makes a wise man better, and a fool worse." Thomas Fuller

Honk if you love Jesus. Text while driving if you want to meet him. Unknown,

"If you drink, don't drive. Don't even putt." Dean Martin

"Travel and change of place impart new vigor to the mind." Seneca

Things to Say & Not Say

If you cannot say something nice, don't say anything at all. That is what my grandmother used to tell us grandkids. It is good advice at any age, time or place. This chapter may seem "obvious", but I would rather ere on the side of stating the obvious and reemphasize what is said in some of the other chapters.

This chapter not only covers verbal communication, but also written communication as well.

With verbal communication it is usually easier to discern the tone and context than with written communication. Therefore you must be much more circumspect with what and how you write.

I have written tons of e-mails and text messages that I NEVER sent. In the heat of the moment I would write a cruel and hurtful note, but I then send it to my draft folder. I will wait a few hours to overnight before I consider whether to send or not. Invariably, I edit or in most cases delete the message.

Offering encouragement, words of love and affirmation are always appropriate.

Things to Say

Use Please and thank you early and often - these are the magic words.

Remember to say please and thank you to all people you deal with. This is especially true with family members who we sometimes take for granted.

Tell your spouse you love them, multiple times per day!

Say this in the morning, noon and night. There is no such thing as saying "I love you" too much. You can do this verbally or with notes, texts, or posts.

Learn to say the following and mean it:

- I'm sorry
- I forgive you
- I was wrong

Be tactful at all times

Tactful usually means holding your tongue and not saying anything at all or waiting to say something in private. It also means you should consider your motives.

Praise in Public - Criticize in private

This is good advice for work, family, church and friendship. Praise, encourage and lift them up in public. Hold your criticism for private conversations.

Let your yes be yes and your no be no

Take a stand and do not back down. Decide where you stand on an issue. This is especially helpful when dealing with your children. It can also be very useful at work as well.

Just walk away if you are angry

If angry try to walk away or count to 10 before you say something that you will regret later. I know this is easy advise to give in a book and difficult to execute in the moment. It will take great self-control and discipline. Lashing out is always the easy path to take. Choose to take the high road.

These are all good things to say:

- Any words of encouragement
- I love you
- I need you
- You are the best
- You are the one for me
- You can do it!
- I believe in you
- We will get through this together
- I love the way you look
- I love you no matter what
- I am here for you

Things not to say

Do not offer unsolicited opinions.

Be quick to offer your opinion if asked, but as a general rule, unsolicited advice and opinions are not usually welcomed.

Do not ask a woman if she is pregnant

Unless you already know the answer to the question

If you cannot say something nice, do not say anything at all.

Good ancient advice that is passed down from generation to generation

Insulting someone and calling it the truth is rude

Learn to be tactful with your comments and opinions. You can disagree without being disagreeable.

Don't call their baby ugly

Nobody wants to hear their baby is ugly. Keep your opinion to yourself. No mother or father thinks their baby is ugly - even though there are some very ugly babies.

Do not be a gossip!

Someone who will gossip to you will gossip about you

Nobody wants to hear that they are fat, stupid or ugly

It is never necessary to be unkind and cruel.

Do not insult the local sports team.

If you are in New England, they LOVE their Patriots. They do not care to hear your opinion about their beloved team. Find other common ground that you can amicably discuss.

Yelling as a general rule is not an appropriate way to have a conversation

I have never seen an effective conversation take place when either party is yelling

Just because a thought enters your mind does not mean you need to share it!

Sometimes it is much better to keep your thoughts to yourself.

Do not start a conversation with " You always or You never"

Using these statements will only lead to a circular argument and you will never get to your point of what you want to discuss.   Avoid using these declarative comments at all costs.

Do not compare your spouse to their parents (in the negative of course).

Telling you bride "You _____ just like your mother".   Don't go down this road.

These are all bad things to say:

- Any Profanity
- I hate you
- You are - stupid, ignorant, idiot
- You are ugly
- You are fat
- You are a waste of time
- You are the worst
- You will never be able to do it!
- I do not believe in you
- I hate the way you look
- "Whatever" this comment is just rude and dismissive

Quotes on Things to Say/Not to Say

"Remember not only to say the right thing in the right place, but far more difficult still, to leave unsaid the wrong thing at the tempting moment." **Ben Franklin**

"Speak only if it improves upon the silence." **Mahatma Gandhi**

"Tact is the art of making a point without making an enemy." **Isaac Newton**

"Don't flatter yourselves that friendship authorizes you to say disagreeable things to your intimates. On the contrary, the nearer you come into relation with a person, the more necessary do tact and courtesy become." **Oliver Wendell Holmes, Sr.**

"Tact is the ability to describe others as they see themselves." **Abraham Lincoln**

"Give thy thoughts no tongue, nor any unproportioned thought his act. Be thou familiar but by no means vulgar." **William Shakespeare**

"It is tact that is golden, not silence." **Samuel Butler**

"Take time to be kind and to say 'thank you." **Zig Ziglar**

"To speak and to speak well are two things. A fool may talk, but a wise man speaks." **Ben Jonson**

"By swallowing evil words unsaid, no one has ever harmed his stomach." **Winston Churchill**

The kindest word in all the world is the unkind word, unsaid. **Unknown**

Even a fish wouldn't get into trouble if he kept his mouth shut. **Unknown**

"Once a word has been allowed to escape, it cannot be recalled."
Horace

Not the fastest horse can catch a word spoken in anger.
Chinese Proverb

Bible Verses on Things to Say/Not to Say

Colossians 4:6
Let your speech always be with grace, as though seasoned with salt, so that you will know how you should respond to each person.

Ephesians 4:29
Let no unwholesome word proceed from your mouth, but only such a word as is good for edification according to the need of the moment, so that it will give grace to those who hear.

Ecclesiastes 10:12
12 Words from the mouth of a wise man are gracious, while the lips of a fool consume him;

Ephesians 5:4
4 and there must be no filthiness and silly talk, or coarse jesting, which are not fitting, but rather giving of thanks.

Colossians 3:8
8 But now you also, put them all aside: anger, wrath, malice, slander, and abusive speech from your mouth.

1 Thessalonians 5:11
11 Therefore [a]encourage one another and build up one another, just as you also are doing.

Proverbs 10:32
32 The lips of the righteous bring forth what is acceptable,
But the mouth of the wicked what is perverted.

Proverbs 18:7
A fool's mouth is his ruin, And his lips are the snare of his soul.

Proverbs 10:14
Wise men store up knowledge, But with the mouth of the foolish, ruin is at hand.

Peace, Rest and Relaxation

Rest seems to a be four letter word these days! People seem to relate rest with slothfulness, but they are not the same. A good physician will tell you that to heal an injury, you need rest. Society today is GO, GO, GO and having your children involved in every imaginable activity.   The problem that I see is that many of these activities are not bad or hurtful; they are just a "time suck" and the family never has time to rest and relax.

The dumbest thing I hear at work is my fellow associates who seem to brag that they are so busy that they never can take all of their vacation. What bunch of baloney! I don't know who they think they are trying to impress, but I feel sorry for them. My company allows me to buy an extra week of vacation and I wish I could buy many more!! I have learned to take all of my vacation time as well as completely disconnecting from work. I believe it is rude and disrespectful to my family for me to continue to work while we are on vacation. I should be paying attention to them.

Invest in creating memories

One of the things we learned from those older and wiser than us, was that we needed to create family memories. The reason for this is that by doing things that created memories, you had that shared experience and bonding.   It gives you something to reminisce about when you gather during the holidays and will also be something for your kids to remember when you are dead and gone.

We never thought of vacations as an expense. It was always considered an investment in memories and experience. Whether it was camping and fishing, a trip to a theme park or hanging out at the beach. We saved the money to invest in these times.

As my children have aged, we have seen them start to invest and create their own memories and do those things that are worth remembering. My oldest daughter has actually thanked us for dragging her into the woods as a child. She now has a love and appreciation for Gods great creation and can now share and enjoy that with others.

Learn to take naps

The power of the nap! It is awesome and you should learn to embrace the greatness of the nap. Naps are not just for toddlers anymore. A 20 to 30 minute can be very refreshing.

Stop often to smell the roses

This is something that I have learned from my bride. When I was younger and dumber, I would rush my family to our vacation destination with little thought as to what we were passing by on our way there or anything else for that matter. I was on a mission to get to our destination.

What I have found is that it is just as much fun to smell the roses and slow down a little bit. Now we stop early and often for ice cream (something we all love). We are just as likely to stop at a yard sale or interesting store these days. Life is just not rushing from place to place. Take the opportunity to slow down and see what is going on around you. You just might have some fun.

Have a hobby, but do not let it control your life

I think everybody should have a hobby of some sort. It is a way to do that one thing that you really love and connects with who you are and your passions. The danger is in letting your hobby become your life. Always be aware of the costs in terms of money and time and the impact on your family.

Take all of your vacation time and disconnect from your job

I actually have people I work with who brag about working so hard they cannot take all of their vacation. I know a Greek word to describe them - idiots!

If you have vacation time, take it all - take it early and often.

I can promise you this. You employer will be more than happy if you did not take your time off. They are not interested in what is best for you and your family. You have earned the time off, take it.

Even more important is to disconnect from work while you are away. Your family needs to know that they are a priority when you are with them. If you are constantly on your phone or computer while you are on vacation, you might as well have stayed at work.

When I go on vacation, I always have someone at work who people can contact if they have a question or task - in other words, I have given myself permission to take time off and be disconnected.

As for my phone and computer - I turn them off , put them in plastic bags and store them in my basement. They never get touched or used until my first day back at work.

I challenge you to leave work at work and invest that precious time with you family. Your job is just not that important.

Find time to rest and reflect

Only you can do this. Nobody else is going to create this time for you. We live lives that are completely wired and connected and this is the new normal for most people. Pull the plug and completely disconnect and take time to think and reflect. This was much easier before cell phones, computers and the internet.

My bride and I get away at least once per year for a few days and completely disconnect. It is a wonderful time for us to enjoy each other and just rest and relax. Try it, it is wonderful

Never make a critical decision when you are tired. If possible, sleep first, eat and them make the decision.

We follow this all the time. Just the other day, by daughter needed to make an important decision about an internship. It would not be an easy choice and the news had come to us late in the day. We discussed the options and then agreed to sleep on it and choose the next day. We were able to make a much better decision with clear minds and full stomachs.

Make your home a place of peace and tranquility

Life and work are too hard to come home to chaos and trouble. Strive to make your home a sanctuary of peace and tranquility. This will take work and effort, but the payoff is worth it!

Use the magic button on your phone that will allow you to rest

It is called the **OFF** button. I challenge you to use it! I use it on my phone all the time! It is a wonderful and glorious feeling to turn it off.

There are also degrees of disconnection you can go through if you cannot bring yourself to turn your phone off completely: Most smart phones can easily do the following:

- Try just turning off your e-mail but leave the phone active.
- Turn off your e-mail as well and set you phone to only ring for family and friends
- Turn off the phone completely

Quotes on Peace, Rest & Relaxation

"Tension is who you think you should be. Relaxation is who you are."
Chinese Proverb

"A good laugh and a long sleep are the best cures in the doctor's book." **Irish Proverb**

"Every now and then go away, have a little relaxation, for when you come back to your work your judgment will be surer. Go some distance away because then the work appears smaller and more of it can be taken in at a glance and a lack of harmony and proportion is more readily seen."   **Leonardo Da Vinci**

"The mind should be allowed some relaxation, that it may return to its work all the better for the rest."   **Seneca**

"Tension is who you think you should be. Relaxation is who you are."
Chinese Proverb

"Take rest; a field that has rested gives a bountiful crop."   **Ovid**

"It is requisite for the relaxation of the mind that we make use, from time to time, of playful deeds and jokes."   **St. Thomas Aquinas**

"How beautiful it is to do nothing, and then to rest afterward."
Spanish Proverb

"If a man insisted always on being serious, and never allowed himself a bit of fun and relaxation, he would go mad or become unstable without knowing it."   **Herodotus**

"What is the answer to this fatigue? Relax! Relax! Relax! Learn to relax while you are doing your work!"   **Dale Carnegie**

"Fatigue makes cowards of us all." **Vince Lombardi**

"He that can take rest is greater than he that can take cities."
Ben Franklin

"What is without periods of rest will not endure." **Ovid**

"He who has peace of mind disturbs neither himself nor another."
Epicurus

"Better than a thousand hollow words, is one word that brings peace."
Buddha

"Peace is not absence of conflict, it is the ability to handle conflict by peaceful means." **Ronald Reagan**

"Peace is costly but it is worth the expense" **African proverb**

"Learn to relax. Your body is precious, as it houses your mind and spirit. Inner peace begins with a relaxed body." **Norman Vincent Peale**

"No matter how much pressure you feel at work, if you could find ways to relax for at least five minutes every hour, you'd be more productive." **Dr. Joyce Brothers**

"Tension is who you think you should be. Relaxation is who you are."
Chinese Proverb

"If a man insisted always on being serious, and never allowed himself a bit of fun and relaxation, he would go mad or become unstable without knowing it." **Herodotus**

Bible Verses on Peace, Rest & Relaxation

Genesis 2:2
By the seventh day God completed His work which He had done, and He rested on the seventh day from all His work which He had done.

Matthew 11:28-30
"Come to Me, all who are weary and heavy-laden, and I will give you rest. Take My yoke upon you and learn from Me, for I am gentle and humble in heart, and you will find rest for your souls. For My yoke is easy and My burden is light."

Exodus 34:21
"You shall work six days, but on the seventh day you shall rest; even during plowing time and harvest you shall rest.

Exodus 33:14
And He said, "My presence shall go with you, and I will give you rest."

Psalm 4:8
In peace I will [a]both lie down and sleep,
For You alone, O Lord, make me to dwell in safety.

2 Thessalonians 3:16
Now may the Lord of peace Himself continually grant you peace in every circumstance. The Lord be with you all!

Philippians 4:6
Be anxious for nothing, but in everything by prayer and supplication with thanksgiving let your requests be made known to God.

John 16:33
These things I have spoken to you, so that in Me you may have peace. In the world you have tribulation, but take courage; I have overcome the world."

1 Peter 5:7
Casting all your anxiety on Him, because He cares for you.

Matthew 5:9
"Blessed are the peacemakers, for they shall be called sons of God.

Romans 12:18
If possible, so far as it depends on you, be at peace with all men.

Hebrews 12:14
Pursue peace with all men, and the sanctification without which no one will see the Lord.

John 14:27
Peace I leave with you; My peace I give to you; not as the world gives do I give to you. Do not let your heart be troubled, nor let it be fearful.

Romans 8:6
For the mind set on the flesh is death, but the mind set on the Spirit is life and peace,

Fear/Doubt/Failure

It is not "if" you will have fear, doubt or failure in your life. It is what you choose do to when you confront these issues.   Below are a few suggestions on dealing with these

Deal with your failure in a positive way

Learn from your mistakes and push forward. Tomorrow will be a new day.

Attitude is everything

You are not a failure unless you choose to be a failure.   You do not always get to choose your circumstances, but you can choose your attitude. A positive attitude can help you overcome fear and failure and also help to influence others as well.

Face your fears head on do not give in to them

Do not hold back because of fear or failure.   Many people are paralyzed by fear and failure. Choose early in your life to be an overcomer.

Surround yourself with people who will encourage you

Having a strong support group is a key foundational item for confronting fear and failure. Avoid people who are only going to contribute to a poor attitude or who will just whine and not help.

Most of the things you fear and worry about will never happen

Most of us worry about "what if" and then never take action or move forward. Most of the things we worry about never come to fruition. Therefore, move forward with confidence that your fears are unfounded.

The greatest distance you will ever travel is the six inches between your ears. By this I mean our fears and doubts are in our brain and mind and we have to conquer them there.

Have someone in your life who can offer perspective and challenge you.

If you are in the depths of despair, you might not be able to "see the forest for the trees". You need someone in your life that is wise enough to see beyond the current crisis and offer a good perspective on how to overcome the issue. You also want someone who will not be afraid to challenge you when you are paralyzed or making poor choices.

Embrace failure and know it is a key component of Growing

The sooner you learn to embrace failure and determine in you r mind that it is a learning experience, the quicker you will rebound to bigger and better things. Failure is a key stepping stone to success.

If God is for us, who can be against us?

This is Romans 8:31! Memorize this scripture

Romans 8:31
.... God is for us, who is against us?

Quotes on Fear/Doubt/Failure

"Don't tell God how Big your storm is, tell the Storm how Big your God is." **Unknown**

"Never let success get to your head, and never let failure get to your heart." **Unknown**

"The only thing we have to fear is fear itself - nameless, unreasoning, unjustified, terror which paralyzes needed efforts to convert retreat into advance." **Franklin D. Roosevelt**

"Fear is a self-imposed prison that will keep you from becoming what God intends for you to be. You must move against it with the weapons of faith and love." **Rick Warren**

"Fear is never a reason for quitting; it is only an excuse "
Norman Vincent Peale

"Fear is only as deep as the mind allows". **Japanese Proverb**

"Fear is pain arising from the anticipation of evil." **Aristotle**

"Failure isn't fatal, but failure to change might be" **John Wooden**

"Fear is the enemy of logic." **Frank Sinatra**

"Fear makes the wolf bigger than he is." **German Proverb**

"Every adversity, every failure, every heartache carries with it the seed of an equal or greater benefit." **Napoleon Hill**

"Where the fear is, happiness is not." **Seneca**

"The only limit to our realization of tomorrow will be our doubts of today." **Franklin D. Roosevelt**

"Our doubts are traitors and make us lose the good we oft might win by fearing to attempt." **Shakespeare**

"The brave man is not he who does not feel afraid, but he who conquers that fear." **Nelson Mandela**

"If you are distressed by anything external, the pain is not due to the thing itself, but to your estimate of it; and this you have the power to revoke at any moment." **Marcus Aurelius**

"Inaction breeds doubt and fear. Action breeds confidence and courage. If you want to conquer fear, do not sit home and think about it. Go out and get busy." **Dale Carnegie**

"I'm not afraid of storms, for I'm learning how to sail my ship." **Louisa May Alcott**

"Don't let the fear of striking out hold you back." **Babe Ruth**

"Avoiding danger is no safer in the long run than outright exposure. The fearful are caught as often as the bold." **Helen Keller**

"Always do what you are afraid to do." **Ralph Waldo Emerson**

"Do the thing you fear to do and keep on doing it...that is the quickest and surest way ever yet discovered to conquer fear." **Dale Carnegie**

"Feed your faith and your fears will starve to death." **Max Lucado**

"I failed my way to success." **Thomas Edison**

"You'll always miss 100% of the shots you don't take." **Wayne Gretzky**

"No man ever achieved worth-while success who did not, at one time or other, find himself with at least one foot hanging well over the brink of failure." **Napoleon Hill**

"Success is most often achieved by those who don't know that failure is inevitable." **Coco Chanel**

"Our greatest glory is not in never falling, but in rising every time we fall." **Confucius**

It's not how far you fall, but how high you bounce that counts."
Zig Ziglar

"Failure is success if we learn from it." **Malcolm Forbes**

"Never be afraid to try something new. Remember, amateurs built the ark; professionals built the Titanic." **Anonymous**

"Failure is a detour, not a dead-end street." **Zig Ziglar**

"Only those who dare to fail greatly can ever achieve greatly."
Robert F. Kennedy

"The only real failure in life is not to be true to the best one knows."
Buddha

"Success is not final, failure is not fatal: it is the courage to continue that counts." **Winston Churchill**

"Failure is only the opportunity to begin again, only this time more wisely." **Henry Ford**

"Develop success from failures. Discouragement and failure are two of the surest stepping stones to success." **Dale Carnegie**

"One who fears failure limits his activities. Failure is only the opportunity to more intelligently begin again." **Henry Ford**

"My great concern is not whether you have failed, but whether you are content with your failure." **Abraham Lincoln**

"Do not fear mistakes. You will know failure. Continue to reach out."
Benjamin Franklin

"Everything you want is on the other side of fear." **Jack Canfield**

"Success is the ability to go from failure to failure without losing your enthusiasm." **Winston Churchill**

"Failures are finger posts on the road to achievement." **C.S. Lewis**

"Remember that failure is an event, not a person." **Zig Ziglar**

"Failure is not falling down, but refusing to get up" **Chinese Proverb**

Bible Verses on Fear/Doubt/Failure

2 Timothy 1:7
For God has not given us a spirit of timidity, but of power and love and discipline.

Isaiah 41:10
'Do not fear, for I am with you;
Do not anxiously look about you, for I am your God.
I will strengthen you, surely I will help you,
Surely I will uphold you with My righteous right hand.'

Philippians 4:6-7
Be anxious for nothing, but in everything by prayer and supplication with thanksgiving let your requests be made known to God. And the peace of God, which surpasses all comprehension, will guard your hearts and your minds in Christ Jesus.

Psalm 23:4
Even though I walk through the valley of the shadow of death,
I fear no evil, for You are with me; Your rod and Your staff, they comfort me.

Matthew 6:34
"So do not worry about tomorrow; for tomorrow will care for itself. Each day has enough trouble of its own.

Psalm 27:1
The Lord is my light and my salvation;
Whom shall I fear?
The Lord is the [a]defense of my life;
Whom shall I dread?

Psalm 46:1
God is our refuge and strength,
A very present help in trouble.

Psalm 34:4

I sought the Lord, and He answered me,
And delivered me from all my fears.

Psalm 118:6-7

The Lord is for me; I will not fear;
What can man do to me?
The Lord is for me among those who help me;
Therefore I will look with satisfaction on those who hate me.

Joshua 1:9

Have I not commanded you? Be strong and courageous! Do not tremble or be
dismayed, for the Lord your God is with you wherever you go."

Proverbs 29:25

The fear of man brings a snare,
But he who trusts in the Lord will be exalted.

1 Peter 5:7

casting all your anxiety on Him, because He cares for you.

The Home

Owning a home is a great investment and sure beats paying rent. If you can afford a home, then make the time to take care of your investment by doing preventive maintenance and fixing things yourself.

Remember when you buy a home, you need to budget a couple hundred dollars extra per month for minor accidents and maintenance, as well as money for the extra tools or supplies you will need to keep your house fixed up. In your first years of home ownership you will need to budget more since you probably won't have all the tools you need yet.

Find a good plumber, electrician and HVAC person

Just like finding a good doctor or dentist to take care of your body, you want to find the right people to take care of you house as well. You will want to find ones that are reliable and more importantly available! Things in the house have a way of breaking down at the most inconvenient time (usually nights and weekends)

Use YouTube® and the internet to fix many common household problems

Before you call the plumber, electrician or HVAC person, go to the internet and see if there is an easy fix first. More time than not, you can save yourself a ton of money by doing it yourself.

Leave a spare key accessible

It is not "if" you will lock yourself out of your house, it is a matter of "when". Go ahead and hide a key somewhere on your property that is easy for you to know and remember and but difficult for someone else.

Change the air filter in your home frequently

This is a good way to prolong the health of your heating and air systems. I do this every 2-3 months.

Change the batteries in the smoke detectors every time we have Day Lights Saving

This is just an easy way to remember when to change the batteries. It is a small thing, but you always want to play it safe with your home and family.

Don't throw grease down the drain

If you throw grease down the drain, it WILL clog up your drain eventually and will cost you ton of money to get cleaned out. Just collect the grease (from various meats that you cook) in a container and throw it out with the trash.

Turn off as many things as you can when you go on vacation

This will save you a lot of money on electricity and utilities. Also shut the water off, so the house does not flood.

Have the means to protect your home and property

Yes I mean a gun. Either a hand gun or shotgun. You are responsible for your own safety. The police will never get there in time.

1. Learn how to properly use your guns. Take lessons.

2. Teach your spouse how to use it

3. Keep it accessible, but safe from children - this is just common sense, but it is also the law in many places. **NEVER** leave a loaded gun in a place where a child can reach and use it. Invest in the right equipment to keep the gun accessible but safe.

4. Go to the firing range to stay up to speed and test your guns a couple of times a year.

5. Do not get a gun unless you are really prepared to use it!

Have a good set of tools available and learn how to use them

Buy really good tools when you are young and they will last you your entire life. Tools you will need:

- Set of socket wrenches
- Power Drill
- Hammer
- Various screw drivers - flat head and Philips head
- Open ended wrenches
- Hack saw
- Ladder
- Extension cord (buy both a short and long one)
- Various plyers
- Tool box
- Flashlight
- Pipe wrench
- Yard tools - shovel, rake, hoe, pick axe, sledge hammer
- A good pair of leather work gloves

These are just the basic tools to get you started.   You will find over time that you your tool collection will grow.

My grandfather always told me. "No job is difficult if you have the right tool." He was absolutely right. Invest in the right tools and you will almost never be sorry

Rent tools and equipment you will not use very often

There is no need to buy a log splitter if you will only use it once a year or every few years. You can rent one for a day, and split all the wood you need. This is true of any tool you will not use often (a chain saw is another tool most people will not use often)

Find the main water shut off to your house (this goes for Gas/Oil and electricity also)

If you have a pipe burst or other water disaster, you will want to quickly be able to shut off the water. When you first buy your home, be sure to find this and make sure everybody in the family knows where it is and how to turn off the water.

Have any trees that are too close to your house taken down

The last thing you want is a tree that may already be leaning towards you house, falling through the roof during a storm. Also, if you have a tree on your property that is leaning towards your neighbor, you can be liable for any damage to their house. Have those trees removed as well.

This is a job left to professionals. So if you do not cut down trees for a living, spend the money to have the professionals do the job.

Call 811 before you dig around your property

This is a service that will come out to your home and mark all underground lines for free. Take advantage of this service. It is a huge free benefit and could save a life! (There are power cables that you do not want to cut through).

Keep all of your owner's manuals in one place

All of your home equipment, appliances and tools have owner's manuals. I have a sturdy plastic container in my basement and keep all of the together. This way, they are easy to find, use and access. This will save you time when something breaks down.

Have as large a deductible as you can tolerate on your homeowners policy.

I would recommend $1,000 minimum deductible and even as high as $5,000 or even $10,000. You will save a ton of money on insurance premium and you should only really be covering yourself for a disaster anyway. The key is having the deductible amount in a savings account to cover the expense when it happens.

Have a fireproof & waterproof safety box for all of your important papers

This will save you a lot of headache and heartache in case of a fire or water damage. The best solution is to actually have a safe deposit box at your local bank.

If it uses gasoline - make sure to crank it up at least once per month

You might have many types of gasoline engine powered equipment. I have a lawnmower, edger, weed eater, generator, and chain saw.   At the end of each season I drain the gas out and run the engine until it stops.   This will help keep the carburetor from clogging up with non-use (this is caused by the ethanol in the fuel we use).

For my generator, I crank it up on the last day of each month to keep the battery charged and to make sure it is good to go.   It would be of little use to have a generator that does not work in an emergency.

If you store gasoline make sure you put a fuel stabilizer in the fuel to keep it fresh.   Gasoline goes stale rather quickly so this a good preventative measure.

Lock your doors when you leave home

Don't make it easy for someone to break into your home.   Always lock up when you leave.

Have an evacuation plan in case of fire or other emergency

Have a plan and walk through it with your children.   You should have a designated gathering place that everyone goes to. This will make it easier to account for all the people in your household.

Keep a fire extinguisher in the house

It is a good idea to keep a fire extinguisher in the kitchen.   This is the room most likely to have a fire.

Replace your showerheads with low flow showerheads

Many homes do not have the new low flow showerheads.   You have no idea how much water you are using when you take a shower. There are new low flow shower heads that give you good pressure, but use a tiny amount of water. Whether you have a large family or not, you can save real money by putting in these low flow showerheads. They are super easy to replace!!

Learn to cook!

Nobody intuitively knows how to cook. Someone has to teach you or you have to learn yourself. Cooking is actually kind of fun and a great way to save money and my yummy meals for yourself and your family.   Here are a few keys:

- Invest in good cookbooks and recipes
- Find a mentor to teach you how to cook (friends, family, neighbors)
- Take a cooking class
- Watch cooking shows for tips and ideas
- Teach your children how to cook at a young age
- Invest in good pots and pans
- Experiment
- Try and Try again
- Remember this is a skill that just about anybody can learn
- Be patient
- Cooking at home saves money and is great for family time around the table.

Be respectful of your neighbors

- If you borrow tools, take them back (clean them first)
- If you borrow something that takes fuel - refill the tank completely (even if it was only half full when you borrowed it)
- Don't do loud yard work early in the morning or late at night
- Respect the boarders of your neighbor's property (good fences make good neighbors)
- Help out in times of crisis
- Watch out for their house when they are away
- Remember that Jesus said "Love your neighbor as yourself"

Quotes on The Home

"Home is a shelter from storms — all sorts of storms."
William J. Bennett

"The strength of a nation derives from the integrity of the home."
Confucius

"There is nothing like staying at home for real comfort."   **Jane Austen**

"A house is not a home unless it contains food and fire for the mind as well as the body."   **Benjamin Franklin**

"A hundred men may make an encampment, but it takes a woman to make a home."   **Chinese Proverb**

"Home is where the heart is." **Pliny the Elder**

'Nothing can bring a real sense of security into the home except true love."   **Billy Graham**

"Home is the place where, when you have to go there, they have to take you in."   **Robert Frost**

SEX

This subject always seems to be somewhat awkward and painful to discuss, and yet it is a very important subject that has a profound effect on life and marriage. There is plenty of bad advice in the world regarding sex. If we do not want our children to get bad advice, then we need to offer the counterpoint of good advice.

I have so many friends who seem to forget that they were ever teenagers or a young adult with an active imagination and sex drive. Their children become teenagers and young adults and they seem to think that there is no need to discuss the subject because surely their children are not thinking about sex or are ever going to engage in sex.

Yes the nice teenage boy next door does want to have sex with your daughter. Yes your daughter is curious about sex.

Save your virginity for marriage.

Sex is a gift. Wait for marriage and share it only with your spouse

Cosmo (Magazine) - is not the place to look for answers about Sex

Be very careful where you seek advice about sex. To many times people will turn to sources that do not have their best interest in mind. Seek wise advice from someone who is happily married and in whom you trust.

If you cannot ask your parents about sex, seek wise counsel from someone in a successful - long term (20+ years) marriage that you trust.

Sex - the four "E's" - Expectations, Experiment, Encourage, Enjoy

Expectations - Be open and honest about your expectations. Share your feelings, thoughts and desires. Be open and honest.

Experiment - don't be afraid to experiment and try new things. However everything should be mutually agreed upon and both of you should be comfortable.

Encourage - encourage one another and take the opportunity to offer words of love and affirmation.

Enjoy - enjoy one another and be thankful for the wonderful gift of sex. It is meant to be enjoyed and cherished in the context of marriage.

Tell your lover what you like and what feels good

Don't be afraid to tell you spouse what you enjoy and what feels good. Also, don't be afraid to ask them what they like and enjoy.

Be sensitive and responsive

Default to being more sensitive to your spouse and their needs, wants and desires. Be responsive to your spouse and their needs, wants and desires. The act of sex should be selfless and loving. Sex is the literal joining of two to become one.

When in doubt, be gentle

Default to gentle as your starting point. Take your time and be a patient lover.

There is no such thing as too much sex

Just like there is no such thing as to much money, there is no such thing as to much sex. Again, this should be by mutual consent, but engaging each other more often than not will also ensure that desires are met and temptations are kept at bay.

Sex should get better with time

As you get to know one another better, your sex life should improve and quite frankly keep improving with age and experience.

Don't set your sexual expectations from Hollywood movies or videos

Sex as usually depicted in the movies is both unrealistic and many times unwise or unhealthy. Be careful what you watch and view.

Avoid Pornography at all costs

Pornography has no place in a healthy marriage. Set guardrails for your marriage and avoid the temptation to view pornography. Pornography is a dangerous and slippery slope that you do not want in your marriage or household. Nothing good can come from bringing this into your marriage.

Bible Verses on Sex

1 Corinthians 7:3-5
The husband must fulfill his duty to his wife, and likewise also the wife to her husband. The wife does not have authority over her own body, but the husband does; and likewise also the husband does not have authority over his own body, but the wife does. Stop depriving one another, except by agreement for a time, so that you may devote yourselves to prayer, and come together again so that Satan will not tempt you because of your lack of self-control.

Hebrews 13:4
Marriage is to be held in honor among all, and the marriage bed is to be undefiled; for fornicators and adulterers God will judge.

Genesis 2:24
For this reason a man shall leave his father and his mother, and be joined to his wife; and they shall become one flesh.

Proverbs 5:18-19
Let your fountain be blessed,
And rejoice in the wife of your youth.
As a loving hind and a graceful doe,
Let her breasts satisfy you at all times;
Be exhilarated always with her love.

1 Corinthians 7:1-2
Now concerning the things about which you wrote, it is good for a man not to touch a woman. But because of immoralities, each man is to have his own wife, and each woman is to have her own husband.

Etiquette and Manners

There are entire books dedicated to proper etiquette and manners. I just want to focus on what I believe are the most important etiquette and manners advice. While not comprehensive, these certainly cover a lot of ground.

Say please and thank you

I had a manager tell me that the higher I went in the organization, the fewer "thank you's" I would receive. He was correct, but that does not make it right. Go out of your way to say please and thank you to those above you, below you and to your peers. Look for opportunities to say thank you to those who work in the background and are rarely noticed.

Don't forget to say please and thank you to your family and friends. Don't take them for granted.

Write thank you notes

This is almost a forgotten art form. A <u>HANDWRITTEN</u> note is a precious gift of time and thought in this day of instant messaging and social media. It will take a small investment in time and money (to buy stamps), but it is well worth the effort.

Be on time (try to be early)

This is very important! If you are to meet someone at 10:00 am then be there early and do not make them wait or wonder. If you know you are running late - then send them a text or call them to let them know.

Send the back the RSVP (whether you intend to go or not) by the deadline.

If someone is inviting you to an important enough event that requires an RSVP, then please take the time to respond.

Be with the person in the moment and ignore/turn off your cell phone

When you are with someone face to face, that trumps anyone on the phone. Turn your phone off and put it away and choose to focus on the person you are with.

Let other people in ahead of you

This can be true when driving and people want to merge into your lane or it can be at the grocery store when you have a full cart of items and the person behind you only has a few things.

It is never appropriate to be rude

Choose to be kind (which many times means not saying what you are thinking). Another word for this is called Tact!

Remember your table manners

Everyone will appreciate you chewing with your mouth closed, asking to having things passed to you (instead of reaching), and using your utensils properly.

Don't discuss sensitive topics at a public social gathering

While you may wish to talk about politics and religion in your personal conversations, it is better to be polite and avoid these topics in public social gatherings.

Share with others

This is true whether you are an adult or a child. It can be a toy as a child and a lunch table as an adult. Sharing is caring!

Be especially kind to Waiter/Waitress

They work very hard for their money and have enough rude and rough people to deal with each day. Show them kindness and gratitude and tip big for good service.

Learn proper Etiquette when you travel to another country

Don't be the rude foreigner who does not understand or bothered to learn the proper etiquette or manners for that country.

Hold the door open for others

This is true for people with their arms full, with children, the elderly and women. I know this may seem old fashioned to hold the door open for a woman, (and I am certain in some circles even considered an insult.), but choose to be old fashioned and open the door for her.

Do not be monosyllabic - speak in sentences

A proper conversation should contain full sentences and not grunts groans or single word answers. Teenagers seem to be very keen to communicate with as few words as possible (unless they are engaging one of their friends).

People appreciate a firm handshake and eye contact

When meeting others for the first time, provide a firm handshake and look them in the eye as you introduce yourself. Repeat their name back to them to be sure you got it right.

Respect the Elderly

Offer them your seat if they are standing, carry stuff for them, offer to fetch items for them or complete tasks. Remember that one day you will be old!

Make others feel included and comfortable

Bring people into your conversations and make guests and others feel comfortable.

Be a good sport!

Nobody likes a sore loser! Congratulate others when they win.
Nobody likes a braggart! Be humble in victory - there is no need to
belittle or taunt your opponent when you are victorious.

Quotes on Etiquette and Manners

"Manners are a sensitive awareness of the feelings of others. If you have that awareness, you have good manners, no matter what fork you use." **Emily Post**

"I believe that a simple and unassuming manner of life is best for everyone, best both for the body and the mind."
Albert Einstein

"The hardest job kids face today is learning good manners without seeing any." **Fred Astaire**

"Good manners are made up of petty sacrifices."
Ralph Waldo Emerson

"Manners are a sensitive awareness of the feelings of others. If you have that awareness, you have good manners, no matter what fork you use." **Emily Post**

"Good breeding consists in concealing how much we think of ourselves and how little we think of the other person."
Mark Twain

"Savages we call them because their manners differ from ours."
Ben Franklin

"Politeness is a sign of dignity, not subservience."
Theodore Roosevelt

Politeness costs little and yields much. **Unknown**

"A real gentleman is as polite to a little girl as to a woman."
Louisa May Alcott

"Consideration for others is the basic of a good life, a good society." **Confucius**

"The test of good manners is to be able to put up pleasantly with bad ones." **Wendell L. Willkie**

"Good manners will open doors that the best education cannot." **Clarence Thomas**

Courtesy that is all on one side cannot last long. **Unknown**

"To be humble to superiors is duty, to equals courtesy, to inferior's nobleness." **Ben Franklin**

"If a man be gracious and courteous to strangers, it shows he is a citizen of the world." **Francis Bacon**

Anyone can be polite to a king. It takes a gentleman to be polite to a beggar. **Anonymous**

"Better were it to be unborn than to be ill bred." **Sir Walter Raleigh**

"Good manners have much to do with the emotions. To make them ring true, one must feel them, not merely exhibit them." **Amy Vanderbilt**

Manners are happy ways of doing things. **Unknown**

"Manners require time, and nothing is more vulgar than haste." **Ralph Waldo Emerson**

Nothing is more noble than politeness, and nothing more ridiculous than ceremony. **Unknown**

To be a successful hostess, when guest arrive say, "At last!" and when they leave say, "So soon!" **Unknown**

Treat your superior as a father, your equal as a brother, and your inferior as a son. **Persian Proverb**

Bible Verses on Etiquette and Manners

Luke 6:31
Treat others the same way you want them to treat you.

Proverbs 23:1
When you sit down to dine with a ruler,
Consider carefully [a]what is before you,

1 Peter 3:8
To sum up, all of you be harmonious, sympathetic, brotherly, kindhearted, and humble in spirit;

Romans 12:10
Be devoted to one another in brotherly love; give preference to one another in honor;

Ephesians 4:29
Let no unwholesome word proceed from your mouth, but only such a word as is good for edification according to the need of the moment, so that it will give grace to those who hear.

Philippians 2:3
Do nothing from selfishness or empty conceit, but with humility of mind regard one another as more important than yourselves;

Titus 3:1-2
Remind them to be subject to rulers, to authorities, to be obedient, to be ready for every good deed, 2 to malign no one, to be peaceable, gentle, showing every consideration for all men.

Matthew 15:11
It is not what enters into the mouth that defiles the man, but what proceeds out of the mouth, this defiles the man."

Colossians 4:6
Let your speech always be with grace, as though seasoned with salt, so that you will know how you should respond to each person.

Proverbs 22:6
Train up a child in the way he should go,
Even when he is old he will not depart from it.

Ephesians 4:32
Be kind to one another, tender-hearted, forgiving each other, just as God in Christ also has forgiven [a]you.

Philippians 2:14
Do all things without grumbling or disputing;

Camping & Outdoor Living

No advice book written by me would be complete without offering advice on camping and the great outdoors. I grew up as a city kid and never got to experience the great outdoors until I married with children. I have come to love camping and spending time in the woods. We are blessed to live in an area of the country where we can camp year round.

I start this chapter with some of the best advice I read about family togetherness and bonding. It comes from Gary Smalley and Dr. James Dobson. When I was reading their books and trying to become a better father and husband, they suggested two activities that all successful families did together. One was camping and the other was boating.

You see when you do these two activities, everybody is in it together and you experience all the trials and tribulations together. You get rained on together, the squirrels steal your food together, and you capsize the boat together. In other words, you are creating memories and bonding.

Take you family camping & boating to build bonds and memories

Just because you did not grow up doing this does not mean you cannot start. I had no clue how camp or use a boat, but I just learned. It took a while, but it was a blast. We have lots of fun and interesting memories from camping and boating. At a minimum, give it a try. You just might like it.

Take advantage of hiking in state and national parks

Hiking is a great way to introduce your family to the great outdoors. It generally does not cost anything and requires little preparation or equipment for day hiking. I would also recommend designated wilderness areas as a great way to get away from it all as well.

Look for hikes that take you to some place specific like a waterfall or natural bridge. This gives you a specific goal to aim for and is something that you will want to take a picture of and remember.

In Georgia we have dozens of state parks and we have visited most of them. Sometimes we just take a weekend and travel to a couple of state parks to visit and see what is there. We also check out the campgrounds and see if that is some place that we would want to camp at in the future.

Save money and just rent a boat

Most of us can never afford a boat nor do we live on the water. However, you can rent a boat for 1/2 day or full day at most lakes and it is money well spent. Boating is a blast, and you do not have to worry about the upkeep or expense of a boat.

Forget the RV and Camper and use a tent

I am just a huge advocate of tent camping. It is less expensive, you can go to many more locations, and everybody gets to help set up. You also have to "rough it" and you just don't get that experience in a camper or RV.

A tent never holds as many people as it says!

If the tent box says it will sleep 8 people, just know that it will only sleep 4 people comfortably! I have a large family (6 of us) and we made the mistake of buying a 6 person tent! Mistake #1. We then traded up to an 8 person tent. Mistake #2. When we finally got our 12 person tent, we were able to comfortably sleep all of us in one tent.

Just buy the bigger tent. You will not be sorry! In the case of family tents, bigger is better!

Use a spare tent as a changing and storage room

We usually take a smaller 4 person tent with us as well as our large family tent. We use the smaller tent to store our clothing and gear, and also use it for changing cloths. Since we have a mix of sons and daughters, this allows for privacy. In addition, the extra storage space means that the main tent only has our sleeping stuff in it and is not cluttered or crowded.

Have a portable potty seat available

We invested in a portable potty seat because one of the most inconvenient things about camping is having to walk to the bathroom in the middle of the night. By having this potty seat with us, we can avoid that trip. My bride says this is her favorite piece of camping equipment!

Borrow camping equipment before you start buying

If you have some friends who will allow you to borrow equipment, try that route first. It will give you a chance to see what kind of equipment you like or dislike.

Be sure to return it DRY and CLEAN.

Buy good quality camping equipment and maintain it

With camping equipment, I have found the quality does matter and so does name brands for the most part. I have spent a lot of money on "cheap" equipment and you get what you pay for. If you have an REI store near you, I would recommend you join and use them. They have superb equipment and a fantastic guarantee program. Also, their staff is incredibly helpful and you can usually pull any piece of equipment out of the box to examine and set up.

Coleman is the "grand daddy' of camping equipment and make excellent stuff as well.

When you buy quality equipment it will last for years, if not decades! I have a ton of equipment that is 20 years old and it still works great. Most likely my grandchildren will be using much of my equipment.

The other key is maintaining your equipment. The biggest mistake people make when they return from camping is that they do not completely DRY OUT and CLEAN their equipment. This leads to rust and mildew and ruins things very quickly. Take the time to properly maintain everything and it will take care of you!

It will rain on you when you go camping

I don't care what the weather service says, you will get rained on!! Just go into it with that mentality and prepare for the rain. Bring rain gear to wear and more importantly, make sure that the seams are sealed on your tent and rain fly. I would also suggest bringing a tarp that is large enough cover your tent.

Sleeping and camping in the rain does not have to be miserable. We have camped in unbelievable storms and stayed dry! This is because I waterproof my tents (even if they say they are waterproof) and I always use an extra tarp for the shade it provides and the extra layer of rain protection.

Use plastic bins to stay organized and keep the animals and weather out

We learned from hard experience that having sturdy plastic bins was a great investment. I purchased mine at Home Depot®. They are heavy duty and stackable. I have had them for 15 years now and they show very little wear and tear. They keep out the rain, bugs and animals. It also does a great job of keeping everything organized.

Pack it in, pack it out

This means do not litter, and bring any trash out with you. Leave the woods and camp grounds nice for the next person to enjoy.

Practice at home first

Never take new camping equipment into the field without practicing using it at home first. You will save a lot of headache and heartache if you follow this simple advice.

Check and recheck all of your equipment before your head out.

Check to make sure you have all the parts and pieces and that everything is working before you head out. This will save you much time and energy.

Start out in State Parks and National Parks near your home

Most states have public camp grounds that are quite tame to use and usually have power and water available at the site. This is an easy way to break into camping. As you progress in confidence, you will want to get father away from civilization and more remote.

Never step into the woods without the following

We never stepped into the woods without the following items at a minimum:

- Knife
- Whistle
- Flashlight
- Ability to Start a fire - lighter, matches and tinder
- Compass and Map

The whole point of always having these few items is that you are setting yourself up for success if you ever got lost. You have a way to stay warm, purify water, signal rescuers, and make a shelter.

We had one of our boys get lost on a hiking trip and he had all of his equipment and followed our plan. When he realized he was lost, he stopped and hugged a tree and started blowing his whistle. We were able to quickly find him because he was prepared.

Being prepared means you have to be intentional and have forethought of your actions and plans.

Hypothermia is real! - Remember, it will be colder than you think

It does not have to be freezing for people to get hypothermia. If you are not properly dressed and prepared you can get hypothermia in temperatures between 40-60 degrees.

What are the warning signs of Hypothermia? Symptoms include confusion, memory loss, drowsiness, exhaustion, slurred speech and fumbling hands.

Dressing in layers can really help with hypothermia. You can take layers off as you heat up with activity, and add layers as you cool down. See the next suggestion.

Dress in Layers to Stay Warm

This is age old wisdom. You are better off with several layers than just a single thick layer. Depending on how cold it is, will depend on how many layers you need (also your body type and temperament). I am warm natured and need less layers, and my bride is cold natured and needs more layers.

Here is a basic suggestion for layers:

- Base layer next to your skin should be soft and moisture wicking. This means it will take moisture away from your body to keep you dry.

- Insulating layers to keep you warm - fleece is an excellent insulating layer.

- Shell layers to keep out wind and water. This layer should be water and wind proof, but also breathable fabric. If not, you will build up sweat and moisture, and it is not as comfortable. Don't skimp money on this layer!!

If your feet are cold, put on a hat

Seems counterintuitive, but it works! Most of the heat from your body escapes through your head and putting on a hat will help retain heat.

Always let others know your plans

Leave a detailed plan of where you are camping or backpacking with someone back home. It is a safe precaution. Especially let them know when you plan to return. This will give them a good indication of when they need to start looking for you if you don't turn up in time.

Never experiment with food while backpacking

Be sure to try all the food you plan to eat on a backpacking trip. There are no stores in the woods, and having bad or nasty food is ZERO fun. Try it all before you take it into the woods with you.

You will need more coolers than you think

Invest your money on coolers that offer 5 days of cooling and have wheels! We generally take three coolers with us. One cooler for drinks, one cooler for "dry food" - stuff that does not need ice but is best kept in a cooler - Bread, chips, PB&J, cookies, etc. Our final cooler is for all the food that does need ice.

You will need more tables than you think

Tables are always a premium when camping. Most campgrounds have a picnic table, but that is it. I would recommend a minimum of two tables, and three is best. You should have one table for cooking equipment, one table for food preparation, and one table for organizing stuff. These should be lightweight folding tables., generally 4-6 feet in length.

You will also find uses for these tables at home as well.

A comfortable place to sit is worth its weight in gold

Invest in some good camp chairs! These are the collapsible type that folds up small and neat, but offer great comfort.

Pre-cook some food to save time and energy

We usually have at least one meal that is pre-cooked and just needs to be heated. For us this means chili, beef stew or taco soup. It is a big time saver and yummy food that everybody loves

Time around the campfire is the one thing everybody loves and will remember

Always have a campfire if possible (it might rain all the time and not make it possible). Time around the campfire is precious and kids love the campfire. Make s'mores and tell stories and sing. Be sure to not let the kids play with the fire and teach them fire safety.

Teach your children how to set up and use the equipment

Even small kids can pitch in and help set up, clean up, cook and prepare. As my kids got older, I had them completely set up the tent and other equipment. It teaches them teamwork, and responsibility.

Have a well equipped kitchen

I would suggest having a box that keeps all of your kitchen equipment together, especially the utensils. Here are some of the key items to include:

- Spatula
- Tongs
- Measuring cup
- Strainer/Colander
- Several types of long kitchen knives
- Large spoons
- Can opener
- Two frying pans
- Multiple size pots
- Insulated cups for hot drinks (unbreakable)
- Large cups for cold drinks
- Forks, spoons, knives
- Propane gas stove
- Coffee maker
- Baking pan
- Pot holder
- Dish towels
- Aluminum foil
- Tub for washing dishes
- Bring paper plates and plastic goods to cut down on things to wash.
- Plastic storage bags and storage bowls

Never camp for less than two nights

Camping for less than two nights is almost a waste of time and energy (unless it is in your back yard). It takes so long to plan, prepare and setup that you will not be pleased with camping only a single night. Three to five nights is the sweet spot for our family.

Learn how to fish

I am not a fisherman and don't know how to fish well. I usually just
end up drowning worms. However, all of my kids love to fish! I
have a sweet picture in my office of all the kids catching their first fish.
We are unsuccessful most of the time, but it is great time none the less.

Use headlamps instead of flashlights

Invest in good headlamps instead of handheld flashlights. The point
of using a headlamp is that it keeps both of your hands free to do
work, and the light is always pointed where your head turns to.

Never go camping without the following equipment

This is not a list of everything you need, just stuff that I recommend for
every camping trip. You will use this stuff.

- A Good hatchet! Spend money on a really good one and it
  will last forever. I actually got mine at Home Depot®.
- Lots for rope - different lengths and types. You will want at
  least one piece of heavy duty rope that is 100 feet long
- Extra tarps - remember it will rain.
- Extra tent stakes - buy heavy duty, long stakes
- Duct tape
- Small shovel
- Multi-tool
- Swiss army knife
- Head Lamps
- Extra batteries for everything
- Extra lighter and matches

Avoid Cotton Clothing when backpacking

While cotton is very comfortable to wear, it has just about ZERO
insulation power when wet, and when it is wet it takes an impossibly
long time to dry. Avoid cotton at all costs if possible - this means no
blue jeans!

Wool socks work well year round

Wool socks are fantastic at keeping your feet warm in winter and dry in the summer. I know it sounds crazy but wool socks are fantastic to wear and your feet will love you for it. The new wool blends they have today are not itchy or scratchy. Invest in some good wool socks (money well spent).

Don't go cheap on your sleeping equipment

Getting a good night's sleep is powerful and refreshing. To make this happen you need to be comfortable. To be comfortable, you will have to invest in good quality equipment.

Do not ever buy an air mattress!! These are a complete waste of money and will leak air!! They do not work long term. We have tried multiple types of air mattresses and they all leak over time.

So what should you buy? Get a self-inflating mattress pad. They are more expensive - but come with a life time warranty. I have yet to have any of these leak air! They are worth their weight in gold. I highly recommend Therm-a-Rest and REI pads. I have one of these pads that is over 20 years old and it is still going strong.

You will then want a good sleeping bag. The key is buying a bag with the right temperature rating. A summer time sleeping bag will be useless in the fall and winter and a winter bag will be stifling in the summer.

We have found that at 20 degree bag is a good compromise bag to use. Be sure to try the bag out in the store before purchasing it. Everybody has a different idea of what a comfortable bag is so you need to try it first. I tend to move around a lot in my sleep, so I don't like a mummy or slim bag.

My favorite piece of equipment for any type of camping.......

A bandana! It has dozens of uses, is small, lightweight and inexpensive. Once you start carrying one, you will never leave home without it.

Equipment I have never regretted purchasing

Here is some of the different equipment that I have never regretted having. You don't need all this stuff, but I love this equipment.

- Propane heaters - you cannot always have a fire and they also provide instant heat (without the smoke)
- Camp oven - one of the more expensive things I have purchased but you can cook and bake so much more. I love making biscuits in the morning
- Thick self- inflating sleep pads - worth their weight in gold
- Huge tarp that covers not only the tent but cooking equipment as well. Offers shade and weather protection
- Dutch oven - very fun to use and impossible to break. My great grandchildren will be using this Dutch oven.
- Small single mantle lanterns. Easier to use then the two mantle lanterns and take up very little room.
- Portable potty seat
- Hammock
- Quality sleeping bags - REI
- Quality tents - REI
- Quality backpacks - REI

If you are lost, stop and hug a tree

We learned this in the Boy Scouts and it is great advice. If you continue to wander around, you will never be found. It is better in most instances to find a place and stay there. If others know you are lost they will more easily be able to find you.

Quotes on Camping and Outdoor Living

"The fire is the main comfort of the camp, whether in summer or winter, and is about as ample at one season as at another. It is as well for cheerfulness as for warmth and dryness. " **Henry David Thoreau**

"In all things of nature there is something of the marvelous." **Aristotle**

"Real freedom lies in wildness, not in civilization." **Charles Lindbergh**

"Climb the mountains and get their good tidings. Nature's peace will flow into you as sunshine flows into trees. The winds will blow their own freshness into you, and the storms their energy, while cares will drop away from you like the leaves of Autumn." **John Muir**

"In God's wildness lies the hope of the world - the great fresh unblighted, unredeemed wilderness. The galling harness of civilization drops off, and wounds heal ere we are aware." **John Muir**

It always rains on tents. Rainstorms will travel thousands of miles, against prevailing winds for the opportunity to rain on a tent.
Dave Barry

"The earth has music for those who listen." **William Shakespeare**

"Look deep into nature, and then you will understand everything better." **Albert Einstein**

"Remember what Bilbo used to say: 'It's a dangerous business, Frodo, going out your door. You step onto the road, and if you don't keep your feet, there's no knowing where you might be swept off to.'"
J.R.R. Tolkien

Ten Words
to Live by

One of my books is titled - _**The 100 Most Important Words**_. The idea behind that book was that I wanted to make sure I was teaching my children these 100 words and pouring into their life the lessons, truth and wisdom to help them grow.

As this book comes to an end, I wanted to include what I believe are the 10 most important words from that book.

1. Intentional
2. Character
3. Faith
4. Hope
5. Love
6. Self-Control
7. Loyalty
8. Generosity
9. Forgiveness
10. Finish

You will note that these words are broad in scope and intended to cover a lot of life situations. These ten words are intended to influence the key aspects of your life: Spiritual, Emotional, Physical, Financial, and Relational.

Intentional

"The choice we face (in life) is between empty self-indulgence and meaningful activity". **Billy Graham**

Definition: Intentional - done in a way that is planned or intended

I wanted to start with the word Intentional. This word has meant so much to me over the past 10 years of my life. It drives the decisions that I make about my time, my talents and my treasure. I tend to be an A++ hyper personality. This means I have a lot going on all the time. If I am not careful, I can lose focus on the most important things in my life if I am not intentional about how I spend my time.

What are those important things in my life: Faith, Family, Friends and Fitness. So how am I intentional in these key areas of my life?

With my faith, it is about having a set time for prayer, worship, study and fellowship. We are in church on Sunday, and back again on Wednesday. I get up in the morning to study and pray.

With my family it is about carving out time each week to focus on different individuals. I have a date night with my Bride, with four children it is very difficult to get that one on one time, so I have set up a weekly routine where Thursday evenings are dedicated to "daddy dates" with my girls and "boys bonding" with my sons.

With our friends, we have been very intentional about inviting both new and old friends over to the house for food and fellowship each month. We are intentional about inviting younger couples whom we can mentor, peers who we can share with and mature couples we can learn from.

With fitness, I have a morning routine of working out with goals and objectives to achieve.

Most importantly, we have been intentional about what we teach our children and the lessons we want them to learn. Parenting is not an adventure for the faint hearted or unprepared.

My challenge to you is as follows:

Consider how you can be more intentional this week in the following areas of your life:

Time - we all have the same amount of time each day (24 hours). How are you going to spend that time? Use a calendar and become very intentional about how you will use your time each day.

Talents - what are the skills and abilities that you have? Are you using them appropriately? How can you be more intentional about using your talents in a positive and meaningful way?

Treasure - this is a tough one for many people. Being intentional about how you spend, save and invest your money will take time and thoughtful effort on your part. If you are not good at this, then I would suggest someone like Dave Ramsey to help (www.daveramsey.com). You must know how each dollar is spent and how you are going to use your money.

If you can consistently be intentional about these three areas of your life, I believe you will find your life much more fulfilling.

Take the opportunity to be more intentional in your life

Homework - take the time this week to look at your calendar and determine how you can be more intentional with your time. If you can better control this one aspect of your life, then you can move on to other areas of your life.

Character

"It was character that got us out of bed, commitment that moved us into action, and discipline that enabled us to follow through".　**Zig Ziglar**

Definition: Character - the way someone thinks, feels, and behaves : someone's personality

Character is something that we are constantly building into our children and something we "harp on" all the time. Character is really the embodiment of some many different qualities: Integrity, honesty, truthfulness, respectful etc. etc.

We know good character when we see it and we know bad character when we see it as well.

When my children were younger we took them to the zoo one day and observed a family of four in front of us. It was a father, mother, teenage boy and a younger sister. They were in front of us in the line to pay for tickets. This is the conversation that we observed:

Father to Attendant: "We need four tickets - two adult and two children"

Son: "But Dad, I'm 14 and it says..."

Father: "Be quiet!"

Son: "But dad you have to be 12 or under to ...."

Father: "HUSH!"

Father to Attendant: "We need four tickets - two adult and two children"

Wow! I could not believe the lessons this father had just taught his children. He had just taught them that it was ok to lie (and I would say sell your integrity), to save $5.00.

I just cannot even begin to imagine the type of character that would be built into those children and especially that son. Since my children had witnessed this entire event, we took the time to sit them down and go over the entire event and explain what was wrong and how we did things in our family.

On another occasion, I had the opportunity to finish the basement of my house so my oldest son could have a room for himself. As we were about to begin construction, I asked my friends and neighbors (many of whom were professed Christians) about their experience and how best to proceed.   To the person, they all told me NOT to apply for building permits (even though that was the law) and to just get the work done quickly and nobody would know.

The reason they all gave me advice for not getting the building permit was as follows:

- It would take additional time.
- The permit would cost money.
- I would have to have everything inspected.
- My taxes would increase.

Needless to say, I did not heed their "advice". And you know what, they were right about every one of those things they called out. It took more time, it cost money and my taxes increased.   But at the end of the day, I could look in the mirror and know I had done the right thing and tell my children (who watched then entire process and have me explain it to them) that our integrity and character was not for sale!

Our children are constantly watching us and want to know if we are going to do the right thing or not!

I have found that many of the instances of lack of character that I see revolve around money is some shape, form or fashion.

How will you build your character this week? Who are you when nobody is looking? Who are you when your children are watching you?

Know this - building character takes time – will it be good character or bad character? The choice is yours!

<u>**Homework**</u> - Choose this day to be a person of integrity in all your dealings (even with the IRS). Consider the verse below and how God would look at your heart.

<u>**1 Samuel 16:7**</u>
But the Lord said to Samuel, "Do not look at his appearance or at the height of his stature, because I have rejected him; for God sees not as man sees, for man looks at the outward appearance, but the Lord looks at the heart."

Faith

"Faith is taking the first step even when you don't see the whole staircase."
Martin Luther King, Jr.

Definition: Faith -strong belief or trust in someone or something
: belief in the existence of God : strong religious feelings or beliefs

In our family it is our faith that defines who we are, what we do, and how we interact with others around us.

We all have faith! When you sit down in a chair you have faith that the legs will hold you up and not break. When you fly in an airplane, you cannot see the air but you have faith that aerodynamics will work and the plane will fly. Most of us have this kind of faith because it is something we can see, feel, touch or have demonstrated to us.

How do you explain faith in God? For me it is quite simple. I know what my life was like before God came into my life through his Son Jesus Christ and I know what my life is like now. I have seen prayers answered and the only explanation is God! I know that sounds simple, but it is childlike faith that God wants us to have!

I honestly do not know how anybody gets through this life without faith in God and the hope for the future. Faith is a very personal and intimate thing! It is something only you can experience for yourself.

Homework - Start today by reading the bible. Start with the New Testament and read through Matthew, Mark, Luke & John and then Romans and Hebrews. In the Old Testament read Proverbs and Psalms. Pray and ask God for his wisdom and discernment to understand the bible and to know Him on a more personal level. See key verses below.

Romans 10:17
So faith comes from hearing, and hearing by the word of Christ.

Ephesians 2:8
For by grace you have been saved through faith; and that not of yourselves, it is the gift of God;

Hebrews 11:6
And without faith it is impossible to please Him, for he who comes to God must believe that He is and that He is a rewarder of those who seek Him.

Hope

"Everything that is done in the world is done by hope." **Martin Luther**

Definition: Hope -to want something to happen or be true and think that it could happen or be true

We use the word hope quite a bit in everyday conversation and thought.

I **hope** he returns my phone call.   I **hope** she says yes.   I **hope** it does not rain.   I **hope** my team wins.   I **hope** the food at this restaurant is good.

The greatest hope we have for mankind is Jesus Christ.   It is only with changed hearts and renewed minds that our hope for the future can be better than our present situation.

I think the hymn - *My Hope is Built on Nothing Less* - by Edward Mote does an excellent job of explaining where our hope comes from.

My hope is built on nothing less
Than Jesus' blood and righteousness.
I dare not trust the sweetest frame,
But wholly trust in Jesus' Name.

Refrain

On Christ the solid Rock I stand,
All other ground is sinking sand;
All other ground is sinking sand.

When darkness seems to hide His face,
I rest on His unchanging grace.
In every high and stormy gale,
My anchor holds within the veil.

Refrain

His oath, His covenant, His blood,
Support me in the whelming flood.
When all around my soul gives way,
He then is all my Hope and Stay.

Refrain

When He shall come with trumpet sound,
Oh may I then in Him be found.
Dressed in His righteousness alone,
Faultless to stand before the throne.

Refrain

Where is your hope?   As for me, my hope is in God and his son Christ Jesus.   He is my firm foundation.

Homework - determine today where your hope lays.   What are you trusting in if not God?

Psalm 39:7
"And now, Lord, for what do I wait? My hope is in You.

Romans 5:3-5
And not only this, but we also exult in our tribulations, knowing that tribulation brings about perseverance; and perseverance, proven character; and proven character, hope; and hope does not disappoint, because the love of God has been poured out within our hearts through the Holy Spirit who was given to us.

Love

"Where there is love there is life." **Mahatma Gandhi**

"Tis better to have loved and lost than never to have loved at all."
Alfred Lord Tennyson

<u>**Definition - Love**</u> - a feeling of strong or constant affection for a person

The English language does a very inadequate job of describing the word love. We have to use inflection, tone of voice and context to convey the type of love we are talking about.   The Ancient Greeks had a much better way of expressing love with different words:

Agape - means love in a "spiritual" sense.

Eros - is "physical" passionate love, with sensual desire and longing. Romantic, pure emotion without the balance of logic.

Philia - is "mental" love. It means affectionate regard or friendship in both ancient and Modern Greek. This type of love requires give and take.

I have an Agape Love for God and my fellow brothers and sisters in Christ.

I have an Eros Love for my Bride

I have a Philia Love for my friends and neighbors.

My life is incomplete without all three types of love evident in my life.   I know that I am a better man for having loved my God, loved my Bride and loved my friends and neighbors.   What a sad and wasted existence it would be in this world without love.

Homework - Where is the love of your life? What do you love most?
Take the time today to show all three forms of love to those around you.

1 Corinthians 13:12-13

For now we see in a mirror dimly, but then face to face; now I know in part, but then I will know fully just as I also have been fully known. But now faith, hope, love, abide these three; but the greatest of these is love

Matthew 22:36-40

"Teacher, which is the great commandment in the Law?" And He said to him, "'You shall love the Lord your God with all your heart, and with all your soul, and with all your mind.' This is the great and foremost commandment. The second is like it, 'You shall love your neighbor as yourself.' On these two commandments depend the whole Law and the Prophets."

Self-Control

"Industry, thrift and self-control are not sought because they create wealth, but because they create character". **Calvin Coolidge**

Definition - Self-Control - restraint exercised over one's own impulses, emotions, or desires

What areas of our life do we need self-control?

Diet?
Exercise?
Prayer?
Discipleship?
Study?
Work?
Internet Surfing?
Social Networking?
Spending?
Saving?
Thoughts?
Speech?
Actions?

Note that I have listed the following: - Physical, Spiritual, Emotional, Financial and Relational aspects of our lives.   The point being that we need self-control in **EVERY** area of our life!!

I find that I can exercise self-control in some areas better than others.   I am a fanatic when it comes to exercise, but eat like a slob!!   I attend church every Sunday, but struggle in my personal devotions and prayer.   I can save money very diligently, but then make a foolish purchase.

What kind of example will you be to your children and your Bride? They will either see evidence of self-control in your life or lack thereof! It is not enough to teach self-control - we must live it out every day in our life.

Homework - make a list of the areas of your life where you believe you exercise great self-control and the reason why you believe you have been successful. Now make an additional list of those areas of your life where you do not have self-control and list the reasons that are holding you back from being in self-control.

Titus 1:7-9

For the overseer must be above reproach as God's steward, not self-willed, not quick-tempered, not addicted to wine, not pugnacious, not fond of sordid gain, but hospitable, loving what is good, sensible, just, devout, self-controlled, holding fast the faithful word which is in accordance with the teaching, so that he will be able both to exhort in sound doctrine and to refute those who contradict.

1 Corinthians 9:24-25

Do you not know that those who run in a race all run, but only one receives the prize? Run in such a way that you may win. 25 Everyone who competes in the games exercises self-control in all things. They then do it to receive a perishable wreath, but we an imperishable.

Loyalty

"Loyalty and friendship, which is to me the same, created all the wealth that I've ever thought I'd have." **Ernie Banks**

<u>Definition - Loyal</u> - having or showing complete and constant support for someone or something

People are very loyal to certain things - sports teams, pets, jobs, relationships etc.

In the South you find out about sports loyalties very quickly!

When I lived in Alabama it was all about - Alabama and Auburn.

When I lived in South Carolina it was all about - South Carolina and Clemson.

When I lived in Texas it was all about - Texas and Texas A&M.

When I lived in Georgia it was all about - Georgia and Georgia Tech.

How do you know people are loyal to their team? They cheer for them whether they win or lose. They wear the team colors and fly flags outside their homes. They have license plates on their cars and key chains with logos.   It is usually not to difficult to know where someone's sports loyalties lie.

Loyalty is an admirable character quality to teach our children.   However, I fear we are too quick to teach them about sports loyalties and not about those loyalties that really matter in life!

Loyalty to our marriage and our Bride! Loyalty to our job and boss! Loyalty to our friends and neighbors! Loyalty to our family!

I encourage you this day to choose to whom you will be loyal and make the effort so that others can see evidence of this loyalty in your life.

Homework - Where do your loyalties lie? Take the time to examine what you are most loyal to in your life and determine if it the really important things our just "stuff".

Joshua 24:15
If it is disagreeable in your sight to serve the Lord, choose for yourselves today whom you will serve: whether the gods which your fathers served which were beyond the River, or the gods of the Amorites in whose land you are living; but as for me and my house, we will serve the Lord."

Proverbs 20:28
Loyalty and truth preserve the king, and he upholds his throne by righteousness.

Proverbs 21:21
He who pursues righteousness and loyalty finds life, righteousness and honor.

Hosea 6:6
For I delight in loyalty rather than sacrifice,
And in the knowledge of God rather than burnt offerings.

Forgive/Forgiveness

"We cannot embrace God's forgiveness if we are so busy clinging to past wounds and nursing old grudges." **T. D. Jakes**

Definition - Forgive - to stop feeling anger toward (someone who has done something wrong) : to stop blaming (someone) : to stop feeling anger about (something) : to forgive someone for (something wrong) : to stop requiring payment of (money that is owed)

Debbie and I could not have survived these 25+ years of marriage without forgiveness. It is just not possible. We see so many couples who are bitter and angry and never learn to forgive. They truly are the ones who are trapped by their un-forgiveness.

For me, the bible is the best source for guidance on forgiveness. The central theme of the Bible is Christ dying on the cross for our sins and all we have to do is ask forgiveness from our sins and God will forgive us because of what Christ did for us on the cross.

If you have not forgiven your spouse for something, then consider these verses and decide if you can still not forgive.

Should we forgive or not?

Matthew 6:14-15 – 14 *For if you forgive others for their transgressions, your heavenly Father will also forgive you. 15 But if you do not forgive others, then your Father will not forgive your transgressions.*

Ephesians 4:32 – 32 *Be kind to one another, tender-hearted, forgiving each other, just as God in Christ also has forgiven you.*

Colossians 3:13 – *bearing with one another, and forgiving each other, whoever has a complaint against anyone; just as the Lord forgave you, so also should you.*

How many times should we forgive?

Matthew 18:21-22 - 21 *Then Peter came and said to Him, "Lord, how often shall my brother sin against me and I forgive him? Up to seven times?" 22 Jesus *said to him, "I do not say to you, up to seven times, but up to seventy times seven.*

Finally – How true Love and Forgiveness go hand in hand

1 Corinthians 13-4:5 -4 *Love is patient, love is kind and is not jealous; love does not brag and is not arrogant, 5 does not act unbecomingly; it does not seek its own, is not provoked, does not take into account a wrong suffered,*

Love keeps no record of wrongs.

Finally, Matthew West has an incredible song called - Forgiveness.   The song was inspired by the story of Renee Napier and her ability to forgive the man who killed her daughter Megan.   Read the words to this song and think about how you would have reacted to this same situation.   I honestly do not know if I would have the courage to forgive the way she did.

Visit their website to read this incredible story.

www.themeagannapierfoundation.com

Homework - is there someone you need to forgive? Do not let anger and hatred eat you alive.   Pray that you would have the courage to forgive.

Psalm 86:5
For You, Lord, are good, and ready to forgive, And abundant in loving kindness to all who call upon You.

Generosity

"Real generosity is doing something nice for someone who will never find out."
Frank A. Clark

Definition - Generosity - the quality of being kind, understanding, and not selfish

The only way I know how to combat my own selfishness, it to be generous! It really is the only antidote to my selfishness.

When most people think about generosity, they think in terms of money and giving. Certainly giving money is a very tangible thing to do and is almost always appreciated.

Remember that generosity is not about the amount given! It is about the attitude and the sacrifice with which it is given. A reluctant or petulant giver or one who is giving out of their surplus is not the type of generous person God is looking for.

Luke 21:1-4
And He looked up and saw the rich putting their gifts into the treasury. And He saw a poor widow putting in two small copper coins. And He said, "Truly I say to you, this poor widow put in more than all of them; for they all out of their surplus put into the offering; but she out of her poverty put in all that she had to live on."

I would also argue that we must also be generous with our time and talents. Time is one commodity that is most precious to everyone and we all have the same amount of time available every day!

Generosity is not only for others. We must demonstrate generosity with our family members as well. Are we giving our Bride and children the time they deserve? Too many times I have spoken with men who said they wished their father has spent more time with them.

Are you using your special talents in a generous way? What are your spiritual gifts? Are you using those in a generous way?

When you do give money is it with a generous heart or is it reluctant? Do you teach your children to give and to do so generously? Do they see you giving generously?

Homework – look for opportunities this week to be generous with your time, talents and treasures. If you can involve your children and Bride so they can see firsthand an example of generous giving.

Proverbs 11:25
The generous man will be prosperous, And he who waters will himself be watered.

Proverbs 22:9
He who is generous will be blessed, For he gives some of his food to the poor.

2 Corinthians 9:7
Each one must do just as he has purposed in his heart, not grudgingly or under compulsion, for God loves a cheerful giver.

Finish

"Finishing well requires tenacity, resolve, and integrity."
Allen Randolph

Definition - Finish - to reach the end of (something) : to stop doing (something) because it is completed

I intentionally wanted to end with this word.

I was at a funeral recently for a woman who was the mother of one of my close friends. Many people talked about the positive impact she had in their lives (both friends and family). At the end, one of her sons came to the front and said "Mom finished well".

What a tribute to a faithful woman!

My pastor has consistently said over the years that he wants to "finish well".

Paul was speaking to his young disciple Timothy when he wrote the following:

2 Timothy 4:7
I have fought the good fight, I have finished the course, I have kept the faith;

It is my desire to finish well! I don't know when the finish line will be reached, so I need to constantly be striving as if the finish line is close.

Homework - we might not all start well, but praise God we can finish well. Begin working today, as if the finish line was very close. We never know how much time we will have.

Philippians 3:14
I press on toward the goal for the prize of the upward call of God in Christ Jesus.

Philippians 1:6

For I am confident of this very thing, that He who began a good work in you will perfect it until the day of Christ Jesus.

Miscellaneous
Advice

Look both ways before crossing the road - this has probably been passed down since the wheel was invented. But if you take this as both a literal road and a philosophical road, it takes on new meaning. As young children, we have to be aware of the dangers in the road, and looking both ways helps us spot the danger that may be coming from either direction. There are many roads we must cross in life - new job, new relationships, conflict, etc. Looking both ways just means to pause before making a decision.

Below is a collection of wisdom, proverbs and sayings that did not necessarily fit into any of the larger buckets of advice. These are in no particular order, so enjoy!

Double knot your shoes before any athletic event

The last thing you want is your shoes flying off in the middle of the competition. I have seen this happen too many times.

Attitude is everything

You cannot always control your circumstances, but you can always control your attitude.

Do your best

In everything you do, you should always put forth your best effort. You will always be glad you did.

Learn from your mistakes

Do not make the same mistake twice. - "Fool me once shame on you, fool me twice, shame on me:

Love is not finite

I know this seems obvious, but I did not learn this until I had children. You think you only have love and capacity for a single child, but you find that you have enough love for everyone!

It is never right to do wrong, and it is never wrong to do right

Not much to explain here.   I have this seared into my mind.   This really is something you should memorize.

If you are not sure - say NO - you can almost always change your mind later

I learned this from a very wise friend of mine.   He was so right.   We have used this many times and have not been sorry yet.

There is more than one way to skin a cat

This just means there is more than one solution to the problem.   If you are stuck, try a different way of solving the issue.   Sometimes the best thing to do is walk away for a while, or step back and think.   To many times we rush when we should think

If it sounds too good to be true, it is!!!!

This is where wisdom and common sense come in handy.   You will be presented with many different offers and opportunities in life.   You will need to be able to discern when it is too good to be true.   Usually this will be presented to you as a "get rich quick" scheme.   Nobody gets rich quick, except those who exploit the foolishness of others.

No one can take your integrity; you can only give it away

Integrity is doing the right thing when no one else is looking. Nobody can take your integrity from you, you can only give it away. Guard your integrity!

Risk more while you are young

When you are young and do not have all the responsibilities of a family or others, take more risks and do some of those things that will be very difficult to do when you are married and older.   It is a small thing to risk a job change early in your career than when you have been with a company for 20 years.

Be a dream maker

Do your best to be a dream maker for your family.   Most of the time this does not involve great expense of money, but will require a commitment of the heart and mind as well as your time. To many times we become dream takers and shot down others dreams and ambitions.   Strive to think of ways to make others dreams come true and how you can encourage them

HALT - learn to know your weakness

HALT is an acronym I learned as a young married man and it has served me well. It is all about decision making and knowing when you are weak and most likely to make a bad decision. If you have any of these four conditions present, then you are in danger of making a poor decision. If you have two or more of these present then you are in danger of making a disastrous or even fatal decision.

Hungry
Angry
Lonely
Tired

When life gives you lemons, make lemonade

Yes this sounds pithy and corny, but it is very true. It is not **IF** life will give you lemons, but **WHEN!** It is your choice as to how you will react.

Do not use your phone on a date or job interview

You would think this is obvious and did not need to be said, but the best thing to do is just turn your phone off and do not let it distract you from the purpose at hand.

You have not because you ask not

To many times people are just afraid to ask for something. You are guaranteed of getting nothing if you do not ask. The worst that can happen in most cases is that you will just get a NO for an answer. Go ahead and ask. - Nothing ventured, nothing gained!

Do not believe everything you read or even see. Especially on the Internet

There is a lot of information out there in many forms. It is very important for you to use different sources to determine what is true and what is not.

Do not take candy from a stranger

This is one of the first pieces of advice we give our children as they start to venture out on their own. However, as adults consider the "candy" that is being offered to you! Beware

Always listen to both sides of the story before passing judgment

There are always two sides to each story (and sometime multiple perspectives if there are witnesses). Gather all the information from all involved before passing judgment. You just might be surprised what you learn.

Always stand up for the weak and defenseless

There is nothing nobler or higher then defending the defenseless! Take courage and know this is **ALWAYS** the right thing to do.

Words mean things

If you really understand this, then you will be very careful with the words you use - whether written or spoken.

Disrespect, Disobedience and Dishonesty are never acceptable behaviors

These three character traits will get you in more trouble, more quickly than just about anything else. Do not accept them in your life or in the life of your children or family.

To thine own self be true - Shakespeare

You can fool other people, but always be honest with yourself.

Opinions are like noses. Everybody has one!!

Be sure that you understand the difference between an opinion and a fact.

"It is cold outside" - this is an opinion

"It is 42 degrees outside" - this is a fact.

Recognize that some opinions matter more than others. The opinion of my Bride matters most to me in life! The opinion of an acquaintance holds little value with me.

The test is not the test, it is your reaction to the test that is the test

You will face many tests in life. If is your attitude and actions towards those test that are the true judge of your character.

You cannot be half pregnant

This is all about commitment!   You are either pregnant or not. There is no in between. Learn to choose sides and be committed.

"80% of success is just showing up" - Woody Allen

There is probably not much wisdom the ever emanated from the mouth of Woody Allen, but this particular piece of wisdom is very true.   So many people just never show up either literally or figuratively. You have to be present to succeed. Fear and despair prevent so many from even trying.

Sports are fun to watch and participate in, but all your passion and energy are should not be completely devoted to sports -

Consider well the sacrifices you are making in a pursuit of your favorite sports team.

Never allow video games or on line gaming in your house.

Just a huge time suck and time waste - not to mention the money wasted!   Get outside!

When in doubt, keep your mouth shut

It is better to be thought a fool, than to open your mouth and remove all doubt. If you are not sure, sit back and listen.

Inspect what you expect

Once you have given clear direction and expectations, it is very important that you follow up to make sure the work is being done correctly.

Do not get involved in any type of gambling

Just like drinking can be addictive, so can gambling.   This means saying no to the lottery, all games of chance, horse racing and other forms of gambling.   If you have to wager anything that you can lose, then that is gambling.   Do not get sucked into this vortex. It is dangerous not only for you, but for your family as well.

Never miss an opportunity to go to the bathroom.

The funny thing about this piece of advice is that it is true no matter how old you are.   However, as we age it becomes even truer!

Hope is not a strategy

I have a good friend of mine who has that on her wall at work and she uses it all the time in meetings!   It is so true that many people wish and hope for a certain outcome, but do not do the work or preparation to achieve that outcome.   You should do all the work and all the preparation and then, and only then, should you hope for the best result.

Always be a generous tipper for good service

Wait staff work hard and long hours with low wages.   They depend on your tips for their income. When you receive good service, remember to be generous with your tips.

Always handle a gun as if it was loaded.

If someone hands you a gun and does not first demonstrate that it is not loaded, then they are a fool. If you take the gun and do not check to see if it is loaded or not, then you are the fool! Always be safe and responsible when handling fire arms.

Practice, Practice, Practice

If you want to improve at any endeavor, you will need to practice more, not less! It does not matter if it is public speaking or shooting a basketball. Practice will give you confidence and better prepare your skill set. If you really study those who are "great", you will find that they practice, practice, practice.

Learn to embrace change

The only thing that is constant is change! Change is something you need to reconcile in your mind that you will not let it affect you in a negative way. No matter what your age or situation in live, change will come at you.

Here are just a few "big" changes that most people will face:

- Move from one school to another
- Get married
- Have children
- Death of a loved one
- New Job
- New boss
- New rules or regulations
- Retire

Most people will say they don't like change. The fact of the matter is t we are faced with change on almost a daily basis. It is your actions and reactions to this change that will affect your relationship with others. Choose to embrace change and "roll with the punches".

Check your teeth in the mirror after eating a salad

To many times I have been caught with salad stuck in my teeth and nobody was willing to tell me. Also, be willing to tell others if they have something stuck in their teeth.

Never sign paperwork without reading it first.

You will constantly be presented with paperwork to sign over the course of your life. Take the time to review the paperwork and read the small print. Once you sign, you are legally bound by its provisions and that could prove to be very detrimental. It will take extra time, but that will be time well spent.

Consult a lawyer if you are confused, unsure or feel pressured to sign anything. Never sign any papers when you are under stress or time pressure.

Other Proverbs, Sayings and Quotes

Below are some additional proverbs and quotes that I wanted to include in the book, but not necessarily expound upon. Many of them should be obvious to the reader. I have listed them in alphabetical order.

A

A bad penny always turns up

A beautiful thing is never perfect

A bird in the hand is worth two in the bush

A chain is only as strong as its weakest link.

A change is as good as a rest

A dog is a man's best friend

A drowning man will clutch at a straw

A fault confessed is half redressed

A fool and his money are soon parted

A friend in need is a friend indeed

A good man is hard to find

A house divided against itself cannot stand

A house is not a home

A journey of a thousand miles begins with a single step

A large chair does not make a king

A leopard cannot change its spots.

A little knowledge is a dangerous thing

A man is known by his friends

A man who is his own lawyer has a fool for his client

A man who uses force is afraid of reasoning

A miss is as good as a mile

A new broom sweeps clean

A penny saved is a penny earned

A person is known by the company they keep

A picture is worth a thousand words.

A place for everything and everything in its place

A poor workman always blames his tools

A problem shared is a problem halved

A prophet is not recognized in his own land

A rising tide lifts all boats

A rolling stone gathers no moss

A soft answer turns away wrath

A stitch in time saves nine

A volunteer is worth twenty pressed men

A watched pot never boils.

A word to the wise is enough

Absence makes the heart grow fonder

Absolute power corrupts absolutely

Actions speak louder than words

Age is honorable and youth is noble

All good things come to he who waits

All good things must come to an end.

All is grist that comes to the mill

All publicity is good publicity

All that glitters is not gold.

All work and no play make Jack a dull boy

All's fair in love and war

An apple a day keeps the doctor away

An army marches on its stomach

An ounce of prevention is worth a pound of cure

Another day, another dollar

Appearances can be deceptive

April is the cruelest month

April showers bring forth May flowers

As you make your bed, so you must lie upon it

As you sow so shall you reap

Ask a silly question and you'll get a silly answer

<u>B</u>

Bad money drives out good

Bad news travels fast

Barking dogs seldom bite

Be an enthusiastic encourager

Be careful what you wish for

Be polite and be fair

Be trustworthy

Beauty is in the eye of the beholder

Beauty is only skin deep

Before you score, you first must have a goal

Beggars can't be choosers.

Behind every great man there's a great woman

Better late than never

Better safe than sorry.

Better the Devil you know than the Devil you don't

Better to have loved and lost than never to have loved at all

Better to light a candle than to curse the darkness

Better to remain silent and be thought a fool that to speak and
remove all doubt

Beware the naked man who offers you his shirt

Big fish eat little fish

Birds of a feather flock together

Blood is thicker than water.

Brevity is the soul of wit

C

Change yourself and fortune will change

Character is always corrupted by prosperity

Cleanliness is next to godliness.

Clothes do not make the man.

Create traditions that your children will want to follow

Curiosity killed the cat.

Cheaters never win and winners never cheat

Cheats never prosper

Cowards may die many times before their death

Crime doesn't pay

D

Dead men tell no tales

Discretion is the better part of valor

Distance lends enchantment to the view

Do as I say, not as I do

Do not boast about tomorrow, because you never know what tomorrow will bring

Do not give in to your fears

Do not worry about what other people think of you

Do unto others as you would have them do to you

Don't sail out farther than you can row back

Don't bite off more than you can chew

Don't bite the hand that feeds you

Don't burn your bridges behind you

Don't cast your pearls before swine

Don't change horses in midstream

Don't count your chickens before they are hatched

Don't cross the bridge till you come to it

Don't cry over spilled milk.

Don't cut off your nose to spite your face

Don't give up what you want most for what you want now.

Don't judge a book by its cover.

Don't judge a man until you've walked in his boots.

Don't leave your manners on the doorstep

Don't let the grass grow under your feet

Don't look a gift horse in the mouth

Don't mix business with pleasure

Don't put all your eggs in one basket

Don't put new wine into old bottles

Don't put off for tomorrow what you can do today

Don't put the cart before the horse

Don't rock the boat

Don't ruin a good apology with an excuse

Don't shoot the messenger

Don't sweat the small stuff

Don't throw the baby out with the bathwater

Don't try to run before you can walk

Don't try to walk before you can crawl

Don't upset the apple-cart

Don't wash your dirty linen in public

Double check your work

Don't run with scissors

Draw from your past, don't let your past draw from you

E

Easy come, easy go.

Everyone is kneaded out of the same dough, but not baked in the same oven

Evil enters like a needle and spreads like an oak tree.

Examine what is said, not who speaks

Every cloud has a silver lining

Every dog has its day

Every Jack has his Jill

East is east, and west is west

East, west, home's best

F

Failing to plan is planning to fail

Faint heart never won fair lady

Faith will move mountains

Familiarity breeds contempt.

Feed a cold and starve a fever

Fight fire with fire

Fight the good fight

Find time to think each day

Finders keepers, losers weepers

First come, first served

First impressions are the most lasting

Fish always stink from the head down

Fish and guests smell after three days

Flattery will get you nowhere

Focus on improving your strengths

Fools rush in where angels fear to tread

For everything there is a season

For want of a nail the shoe was lost; for want of a shoe the horse was lost; and for want of a horse the man was lost

Forewarned is forearmed.

Forgive and forget

Forgiveness is freedom

Fortune favors the bold.

From the sublime to the ridiculous is only one step

G

Get out of the car that is driven by fools

Get out of your own way

Good advice is often annoying, bad advice never is

Good things come in small packages.

Good things come to those who wait.

Give a man a fish and you will feed him for only a day...

Give a man enough rope and he will hang himself

Give credit where credit is due

Go the extra mile

Good fences make good neighbors

Good talk saves the food

Good things come to those who wait

Great minds think alike

Get it working first, then make enhancements

H

Haste makes waste.

He who always thinks it is too soon is sure to come too late

He who does not travel, does not know the value of men

He who hesitates is lost.

He who laughs last, laughs best.

Hindsight is better than foresight.

Hold yourself to a high level of expectations

Honesty is the best policy.

Hope for the best, but prepare for the worst.

Hard cases make bad law

Hard work never did anyone any harm

Haste makes waste

He that goes a-borrowing, goes a-sorrowing

He who can does, he who cannot, teaches

He who fights and runs away, may live to fight another day

He who lives by the sword shall die by the sword

He who pays the piper calls the tune

Hell hath no fury like a woman scorned

Hindsight is always twenty-twenty

History repeats itself

Home is where the heart is

Honesty is the best policy

Hope is not a sound strategy

Half a loaf is better than no bread

He that would eat the fruit, must climb the tree

I

If a job is worth doing it is worth doing well

If at first you don't succeed try, try and try again

If it ain't broke, don't fix it.

If life deals you lemons, make lemonade

It costs nothing to be kind

If the shoe fits, wear it

If wishes were horses, beggars would ride

If you build it they will come

If you can't live longer, live deeper

If you can't beat them, join them

If you can't stand the heat get out of the kitchen

If you lie down with dogs, you will get up with fleas

If you pay peanuts, you get monkeys

If you take big paces, you leave big spaces

If you want a thing done well, do it yourself

Ignorance is bliss

Imitation is the sincerest form of flattery.

In a battle between elephants, the ants get squashed

In love, there is always one who kisses and one who offers the cheek

In the kingdom of the blind the one eyed man is king

In the midst of life we are in death

In unity there is strength.

Instruction in youth is like engraving in stone

Into every life a little rain must fall

It ain't over till the fat lady sings

It is better to give than to receive

It is easy to be wise after the event

It takes a thief to catch a thief

It takes a whole village to raise a child

It takes all sorts to make a world

It takes one to know one

It takes two to tango

It's better to light a candle than curse the darkness

It's all grist to the mill

It's better to have loved and lost than never to have loved at all

It's better to light a candle than curse the darkness

It's never too late

It's no use crying over spilt milk

It's no use locking the stable door after the horse has bolted

It's the empty can that makes the most noise

I

Judge a man by his questions rather than by his answers.

Judge a tree from its fruit, not from its leaves

Just do it

K

Keep a secret a secret!

Keep your eyes and ears open and you mouth shut

Keep it simple

Know your limitations

Keep your chin up

Keep your powder dry

Keep no secrets, tell no lies

L

Laugh and the world laughs with you, weep and you weep alone

Laughter is the best medicine

Learn from your mistakes

Leave well enough alone

Less is more

Let bygones be bygones

Let not the sun go down on your wrath

Let sleeping dogs lie

Let the buyer beware

Let the dead bury the dead

Let the punishment fit the crime

Life begins at forty

Life is what you make it

Lightning never strikes twice in the same place

Like father, like son

Little strokes fell great oaks

Little things please little minds

Live and learn

Live for today for tomorrow never comes

Live in another culture

Look before you leap

Look both ways before you cross the road

Love is blind.

Love makes the world go round.

Love of money is the root of all evil

Love will find a way

M

Make hay while the sun shines.

Measure a thousand times and cut once

Might makes right.

Misery loves company

Money does not grow on trees.

Make hay while the sun shines

Make love not war

Man does not live by bread alone

Many a true word is spoken in jest

Many are called but few are chosen

Many hands make light work

March comes in like a lion, and goes out like a lamb

March winds and April showers bring forth May flowers

Mighty oaks from little acorns grow

Money doesn't grow on trees

Money isn't everything

Money makes the world go round

Money talks

More haste, less speed

Music has charms to soothe the savage breast

N

Necessity is the mother of invention

Needs must when the devil drives

Never go to bed on an argument

Never judge a book by its cover

Never let the sun go down on your anger

Never look a gift horse in the mouth.

Never put off until tomorrow what you can do today

Never speak ill of the dead

Never tell tales out of school

No man can paddle two canoes at the same time

No man can serve two masters

No man is an island

No news is good news

No one can make you feel inferior without your consent

No pain, no gain

No rest for the wicked

Nobody has it all together

Nothing hurts like the truth.

Nothing is certain but death and taxes

Nothing new under the sun

Nothing succeeds like success

Nothing ventured, nothing gained

Not everything is as it seems

O

Old habits die hard.

One good turn deserves another.

One man's trash is another man's treasure

Oil and water don't mix

Old soldiers never die, they just fade away

Once a thief, always a thief

Once bitten, twice shy

One good turn deserves another

One hand washes the other

One man's meat is another man's poison

One volunteer is worth ten pressed men

Opportunity never knocks twice at any man's door

Out of sight, out of mind

P

People who live in glass houses should not throw stones

Possession is nine-tenths of the law

Practice makes perfect.

Pride goes before the fall

Parsley seed goes nine times to the Devil

Patience is a virtue

Penny wise and pound foolish

Power corrupts; absolute power corrupts absolutely

Practice what you preach

Prevention is better than cure

Q

Quality is everyone's responsibility.

Quality is not an act, it is a habit

Quality means doing it right when no one is looking

R

Respect is never given, it is earned

Rome wasn't built in a day

Red sky at night shepherd's delight; red sky in the morning, shepherd's warning

Revenge is a dish best served cold

Rob Peter to pay Paul

S

Seize the day

Shared joy is a double joy; shared sorrow is half a sorrow

Speak the truth, but leave immediately after

Still waters run deep

Strike while the iron is hot.

Success has many fathers, while failure is an orphan

Speak softly and carry a big stick

Spare the rod and spoil the child

Share and share alike

Silence is golden

Seeing is believing

Seek and ye shall find

T

Take care of the pennies and the dollars will take care of themselves

Take each day as it comes

Talk is cheap

Talk of the Devil, and he is bound to appear

That which does not kill us makes us stronger

The age of miracles is past

The apple never falls far from the tree

The best defense is a good offence

The best is the enemy of the good

The best things in life are free.

The bigger they are, the harder they fall.

The bottom line is the bottom line

The boy is father to the man

The cobbler always wears the worst shoes

The customer is always right

The darkest hour is just before the dawn

The devil finds work for idle hands to do

The early bird catches the worm.

The end justifies the means

The first step is always the hardest.

The gap between expectations and reality is frustration

The grass is always greener on the other side of the fence.

The hand that rocks the cradle rules the world

The heart that loves is always young.

The laborer is worthy of his hire

The leopard does not change his spots

The more the merrier

The more things change, the more they stay the same

The most beautiful fig may contain a worm

The night rinses what the day has soaped

The opera isn't over till the fat lady sings

The pen is mightier than sword

The price of liberty is eternal vigilance

The proof of the pudding is in the eating.

The reputation of a thousand years may be determined by the conduct of one hour.

The road to hell is paved with good intentions

The shoemaker's son always goes barefoot

The squeaky wheel gets the grease.

The truth will always come out

The wages of sin is death

The way to a man's heart is through his stomach.

The whole is greater than the sum of the parts

There are none so blind as those, that will not see

There are two sides to every question

There but for the grace of God, go I

There is no honor among thieves.

There is no such thing as too much time, too much money or too much love

There's a time and a place for everything

There's always more fish in the sea

There's an exception to every rule

There's many a good tune played on an old fiddle

There's more than one way to skin a cat

There's no accounting for tastes

There's no fool like an old fool.

There's no place like home

There's no smoke without fire

There's no such thing as a free lunch.

There's no such thing as bad publicity

There's no time like the present.

There's none so deaf as those who will not hear

There's safety in numbers

They that sow the wind, shall reap the whirlwind

Those who do not learn from history are doomed to repeat it

Those who live in glass houses shouldn't throw stones

Those who sleep with dogs will rise with fleas

Time and tide wait for no man

Time and words can't be recalled, even if it was only yesterday

To be willing is only half the task

Time flies

Time is a great healer

Time is money

Time will tell

Time heals all wounds

To whom much is given, much is expected

Too many chiefs, not enough Indians.

Too many cooks spoil the broth.

Try new foods

Turn your face to the sun and the shadows will fall behind you

Two heads are better than one

Two wrongs don't make a right.

Two's company, but three's a crowd

U

United we stand, divided we fall

Unity is strength, division is weakness

V

Variety is the spice of life

Virtue is its own reward

W

What you see in yourself is what you see in the world

When in Rome, do as the Romans

When the cat's away, the mice play

When the going gets tough, the tough get going

When the sun rises, it rises for everyone

Where love reigns, the impossible may be attained

Where there's smoke, there's fire

Who begins too much accomplishes little

Whoever gossips to you will gossip about you

Words should be weighed, not counted

Walls have ears

Walnuts and pears you plant for your heirs

Waste not want not

What can't be cured must be endured

What goes up must come down

What's good for the goose is good for the gander

When the cat's away the mice will play

When the going gets tough, the tough get going

What the eye doesn't see, the heart doesn't grieve over

Where there's a will there's a way

While there's life there's hope

Why keep a dog and bark yourself?

Women and children first

Wonders will never cease

Work expands so as to fill the time available

Worrying never did anyone any good

Y

You always have more options than you think you have

You can lead a horse to water, but you can't make him drink

You can't always get what you want

You can't have your cake and eat it too

You can't judge a book by its cover

You can't make an omelet without breaking a few eggs

You can't teach an old dog new tricks

You have to take the good with the bad

You will reap what you sow

You are never too old to learn

You are what you eat

You can choose your friends but you can't choose your family

You can have too much of a good thing

You can't get blood out of a stone

You can't make a silk purse from a sow's ear

You can't make bricks without straw

You can't run with the hare and hunt with the hounds

You can't judge a book by its cover

You can't win them all

You catch more flies with honey than with vinegar

You pays your money and you takes your choice

You win some, you lose some

Youth is wasted on the young

Your thoughts are limited by your vocabulary

Z

A zebra cannot changes its stripes

Final Quotes

"Rarely affirm, seldom deny, always distinguish."
Thomas Aquinas

"Do not spoil what you have by desiring what you have not."
Epicurus

"It is only prudent never to place complete confidence in that by which we have even once been deceived." **René Descartes**

"Those that know, do. Those that understand, teach." **Aristotle**

"Think no vice so small that you may commit it, and no virtue so small that you may overlook it." **Confucius**

"They, who would give up an essential liberty for temporary security, deserve neither liberty or security." **Ben Franklin**

"We are what we repeatedly do. Excellence, then, is not an act, but a habit." **Aristotle**

"No one can make you feel inferior without your consent."
Eleanor Roosevelt

"Whatever is begun in anger, ends in shame." - **Ben Franklin**

"Twenty years from now you will be more disappointed by the things that you didn't do than by the ones you did do. So throw off the bowlines, Sail away from the safe harbor, Catch the trade winds in your sails. Explore. Dream. Discover." **Mark Twain**

"Content makes poor men rich; discontentment makes rich men poor."
Ben Franklin

"The fear of death follows from the fear of life. A man who loves fully is prepared to die at any time." **Mark Twain**

"A spoonful of honey will catch more flies than a gallon of vinegar."
Ben Franklin

"Anger is never without reason, but seldom with a good one."
Ben Franklin

"Only the dead have seen the end of war." **Plato**

"If you can't explain it to a six year old, you don't understand it yourself." **Albert Einstein**

"We can easily forgive a child who is afraid of the dark; the real tragedy of life is when men are afraid of the light." **Plato**

"Winning is not a sometime thing, it is an all the time thing. You don't do things right once in a while...you do them right all the time."
Vince Lombardi

"Success usually comes to those who are too busy to be looking for it."
Henry David Thoreau

"The greater damage for most of us is not that our aim is too high and we miss it, but that it is too low and we reach it." **Michelangelo**

"Unless a man believes in himself and makes a total commitment to his career and puts everything he has into it – his mind, his body, his heart – what's life worth to him?" **Vince Lombardi**

"When one door of happiness closes, another opens; but often we look so long at the closed door that we do not see the one which has been opened for us." **Helen Keller**

"When you're finished changing, you're finished. **Ben Franklin**

"Once a man has made a commitment to a way of life, he puts the greatest strength in the world behind him. It's something we call heart power. Once a man has made this commitment, nothing will stop him short of success." **Vince Lombardi**

"The good Lord gave you a body that can stand most anything. It's your mind you have to convince." **Vince Lombardi**

"What the mind of man can conceive and believe, the mind of man can achieve." **Napoleon Hill**

"Peak performance begins with your taking complete responsibility for your life and everything that happens to you." **Brian Tracy**

"Impossible is a word to be found only in the dictionary of fools." **Napoleon Bonaparte**

"Perfection is not attainable. But if we chase perfection, we can catch excellence." **Vince Lombardi**

"Be yourself; everyone else is already taken." **Oscar Wilde**

"There never was a good war or a bad peace." **Ben Franklin**

"You know you're in love when you can't fall asleep because reality is finally better than your dreams." **Dr. Seuss**

"It's not who you are that holds you back, it's who you think you're not" **Unknown**

"The only way of finding the limits of the possible is by going beyond them into the impossible." **Arthur C. Clarke**

"It is hard to fail but it is worse never to have tried to succeed." **Theodore Roosevelt**

"People often say that motivation doesn't last. Well, neither does bathing – that's why we recommend it daily." **Zig Ziglar**

"Glass, china, and reputation are easily cracked, and never mended well" **Ben Franklin**

"There is just one life for each of us: our own." **Euripides**

"Friendship is born at that moment when one person says to another: "What! You too? I thought I was the only one." **C.S. Lewis**

"Don't walk behind me; I may not lead. Don't walk in front of me; I may not follow. Just walk beside me and be my friend." **Albert Camus**

"No one can make you feel inferior without your consent." **Eleanor Roosevelt**

"I've learned that people will forget what you said, people will forget what you did, but people will never forget how you made them feel."
 Maya Angelou

"To live is the rarest thing in the world. Most people exist, that is all."
Oscar Wilde

"Remember, happiness doesn't depend upon who you are or what you have, it depends solely upon what you think." **Dale Carnegie**

 "I have not failed. I've just found 10,000 ways that won't work."
Thomas A. Edison

"The only man who never makes mistakes is the man who never does anything." **Theodore Roosevelt**

"Man's mind, once stretched by a new idea, never regains its original dimensions." **Oliver Wendell Holmes, Jr**

"He that lives upon hope will die fasting." **Ben Franklin**

"There are only two ways to live your life. One is as though nothing is a miracle. The other is as though everything is a miracle."
Albert Einstein

"Let others lead small lives, but not you. Let others argue over small things, but not you. Let others cry over small hurts, but not you. Let others leave their future in someone else's hands, but not you."
Jim Rohn

"The secret of getting ahead is getting started." **Mark Twain**

 "Do not go where the path may lead , go instead where there is no path and leave a trail." **Ralph Waldo Emerson**

"Faith consists in believing when it is beyond the power of reason to believe." **Voltaire**

"Some people die at twenty-five and aren't buried until they are seventy-five." **Ben Franklin**

"To be yourself in a world that is constantly trying to make you something else is the greatest accomplishment."
Ralph Waldo Emerson

"For every minute you are angry you lose sixty seconds of happiness."
Ralph Waldo Emerson

"People are just as happy as they make up their minds to be."
Abraham Lincoln

"Life is like riding a bicycle. To keep your balance, you must keep moving." **Albert Einstein**

"Do one thing every day that scares you."
Eleanor Roosevelt

"If you would persuade, you must appeal to interest rather than intellect." **Ben Franklin**

"Being deeply loved by someone gives you strength, while loving someone deeply gives you courage." **Lao Tzu**

"It is never too late to be what you might have been." **George Eliot**

"Not all of us can do great things. But we can do small things with great love." **Mother Teresa**

"To thine own self be true, and it must follow, as the night the day, thou canst not then be false to any man." **William Shakespeare**

"You can fool all the people some of the time, and some of the people all the time, but you cannot fool all the people all the time."
Abraham Lincoln

"If I am not for me, who will be? If I am only for me, what am I? If not now, when?" **Rabbi Hillel**

"Make new friends but stick to old, one is silver, the other gold"
Nursery Rhyme.

"If you want to be happily married, marry a happy person." **Unknown**

"The man who never made a mistake never made anything."
Albert Einstein

"If I had eight hours to chop down a tree, I'd spend six sharpening my axe" **Abraham Lincoln**

"Never argue with a stupid person, they'll drag you down to their level and beat you with experience." **Mark twain**

"Disciplining yourself to do what you know is right and important, although difficult, is the high road to pride, self-esteem and personal satisfaction." **Brian Tracy**

"Make the best use of what is in your power, and take the rest as it happens." **Epictetus**

Final Thoughts

First, thank you so much for taking the time to read this book. It is my prayer that this has been a blessing to you and your family.

Secondly, if you have an opportunity to send me an e-mail with your thoughts, comments or suggestions, that would be very helpful.

paulbeersdorf@gmail.com

Blessings to you and your family!

Paul Beersdorf

www.ingramcontent.com/pod-product-compliance
Lightning Source LLC
LaVergne TN
LVHW051039080426
835508LV00019B/1611